Action Research for Improving Educational Practice

Second Edition

Action Research for Improving Educational Practice

A *Step-by-Step Guide*

Second Edition

Valsa Koshy

Los Angeles | London | New Delhi
Singapore | Washington DC

First edition published as Action Research for Improving Practice, 2005
Reprinted 2006, 2007, 2008, 2009
Second edition published 2010

SAGE Publications Ltd
1 Oliver's Yard
55 City Road
London EC1Y 1SP

SAGE Publications Inc.
2455 Teller Road
Thousand Oaks, California 91320

SAGE Publications India Pvt Ltd
B 1/I 1 Mohan Cooperative Industrial Area
Mathura Road
New Delhi 110 044

SAGE Publications Asia-Pacific Pte Ltd
33 Pekin Street #02-01
Far East Square
Singapore 048763

Library of Congress Control Number: 2009932902

British Library Cataloguing in Publication data

A catalogue record for this book is available from
the British Library

ISBN 0 978-1-84860-159-8
ISBN 0 978-1-84860-160-4 (pbk)

Typeset by C&M Digitals Pvt Ltd, Chennai, India
Printed in Great Britain by TJ International Ltd, Padstow, Cornwall
Printed on paper from sustainable resources

Mixed Sources
Product group from well-managed
forests and other controlled sources
www.fsc.org Cert no. SGS-COC-2482
© 1996 Forest Stewardship Council
FSC

Contents

About the Author

Valsa Koshy is a Professor of Education, at Brunel University. She draws on her diverse experience which includes: teaching and supervizing PGCE, Master's and doctoral students and leading teachers' professional development in several education authorities. She has also supervised a large number of externally funded action research projects, as part of the activities of the Research and Development Centre which she directs. Prior to working in higher education, she was a classroom teacher and, subsequently, was a member of the advisory team of the Inner London Education Authority.

Acknowledgements

I am indebted to many people and organizations for providing me with the opportunity to support practitioners with their action research. I have learnt a great deal from these experiences and this learning has guided me in writing this book. Although it is impossible for me to list all the people who have influenced me over the years, I would like to express my gratitude to all of them. My special thanks to the following:

- The Department for Children, Schools and Families (DCSF) for supporting 14 groups of practitioner researchers, across the country, to research into aspects of a complex and challenging topic – developing the gifts and talents of children aged 5–7. I had the privilege of experiencing the impact of the action research process on their practice and the enhancement of opportunities for these children. This support, provided by funding from the UK government, convinced me of the significant role of practitioner research for improving practice.
- All the practitioners from schools and educational organizations I have guided, over the years, to carry out action research. I have learnt much from my students, at undergraduate and postgraduate levels and, more recently, those who are studying for their Professional Education doctorates (EdD) who have carried out action research as part of their academic work. I have seen, first-hand, the level of enthusiasm, excitement and commitment of these people which has convinced me of the unique opportunities provided by action research for improving educational practice.
- The many children I have observed, who were the ultimate beneficiaries of the action research carried out by the practitioners.
- I am grateful to my two colleagues: Catrin Pinheiro-Torres, for her help and support and for sharing her freshness and dedication to research methodology, in particular for her contribution to the data analysis section; Carole Portman Smith, for her constant encouragement and for demonstrating how practitioners develop through research relating to their work.
- Finally, I acknowledge the contribution of Ron Casey, with whom I launched a Research and Development Centre at the university, and who has been the most influential tutor I have had in my academic career. Discussing educational issues with him and listening to him continually questioning and challenging perspectives, often convinced me of the need for practitioners to reflect on their practices in order to initiate changes with increased understanding and confidence.

Introduction

'Doing a piece of research on how to enhance the learning opportunities of gifted children has been the most rewarding experience of my working life. I secured a grant from a government agency, which enabled me to use action research to design a lens to get my classroom work into focus – magnifying what was good and gratifying, but also highlighting those aspects in need of redirection and rejuvenation. Before that elevating experience I assumed that all forms of research were the exclusive province of academic researchers in universities. Gaining access to that ivory tower has enabled one practitioner – me – to illuminate sound strategies to enable colleagues to navigate their way through the parts of the maze of gifted education.'

Laura, a classroom teacher

I vividly remember Laura's excitement when she secured a grant to carry out an action research project on a topic relating to provision for higher ability pupils, which I had the privilege of supervizing. At the time of obtaining the grant there had been very little research carried out on aspects of provision for higher ability pupils in England and Wales. Laura's interest stemmed from her noticing how bored some children were in her classroom. Comments from an inspection team that the whole school needed to address the issue of more effective provision for very able children confirmed her reason for concern. She carried out the study within ten months, in stages: defining the topic for her research, finding out what was happening in her class and that of a willing colleague, reading around the topic, planning activities which demanded higher cognitive skills, collecting and analysing data, reflecting on her practice, evaluating and disseminating her findings to her colleagues at her school and at the local teachers' professional development centre. My aim in writing this book is to share some of my experiences, such as supervizing Laura's action research, and to generate a set of guidelines for practitioners to enable them to undertake action research so as to enhance their own professional practice as well as to provide leadership to their colleagues.

Similar testimonies to that of Laura's, from practitioners, on the benefits of undertaking action research were reported in the *Times Education Supplement* (2004), appropriately entitled 'Classroom Discoveries'. In an illuminating article, MacGarvey compares teacher researchers to gardeners nurturing new plants and shares her experience of working with teachers who are enthusiastic about practitioner research, are keen to test out theories about learning styles and motivational strategies, and interested in methods of investigation.

In the past few years, action research has become increasingly popular as a mode of research among practitioners who are constantly faced with the challenges of providing effective teaching strategies, raising achievement, exploring pedagogical issues and addressing the special needs of students. The main role of action research is to facilitate practitioners to study aspects of practice – whether it is in the context of introducing an innovative idea or in assessing and reflecting on the effectiveness of existing practice, with a view to improving practice. This process is often carried out within a researcher's own setting. The importance of professional development for enhancing the quality of practice has long been recognized both within the United Kingdom and abroad. Hargreaves (1996) points out that research-based practice would be more effective and satisfying for practitioners.

Action research is quite often used as the method of enquiry by undergraduate and postgraduate students in higher education who are studying for accredited courses. In recent years, students studying for taught doctorate (EdD) degrees with their focus on practical aspects of education have also been adopting action research as a method of study. This book attempts to meet the needs of all the above groups of people by providing a coherent, accessible, and practical set of guidelines on how to carry out action research. However, it also needs acknowledging here that one book alone cannot provide a complete account of all aspects of research. Readers, therefore, are given a list of some authoritative sources and readings for further support.

The contents of this book draw mainly on my personal experience of fifteen years in guiding researchers in various settings – as Course Leader for Master's programmes, as Director of Academic and Professional Development for practitioners in education and also through my involvement in research training for doctoral students at my university. During this time I have also supervized a number of practising teachers who were carrying out funded action research projects. What I have written is also informed by the many conference presentations on action research at national and international research conferences I have attended as well as the increasing number of published articles based on action research.

As the main purpose of this book is to offer practical guidance to those who intend to carry out action research, I feel it is important to ask three key questions:

- What is action research?
- When would it be appropriate for a practitioner to carry out action research?
- How would one go about carrying out action research?

I have attempted to address all of these questions in this book. To start us down the right track, it would be useful to consider why we may undertake action research. Doing action research facilitates evaluation and reflection in order to implement necessary changes in practice – both for an individual and within an institution. As new initiatives are introduced with greater frequency within education policies all over the world, practitioners can often be left with conflicting viewpoints, doubts and dilemmas which in turn need exploration, evaluation and reflection. Evaluating one's own practices is an integral part of an applied discipline such as education.

This book addresses the needs of two groups of researchers:

- Those who wish to undertake small-scale research into an aspect of their practice. This may be facilitated by external funding or may be the outcome of a local necessity to evaluate the effectiveness of an innovation or an initiative. Undertaking an action research project would involve looking at issues in depth and gathering and assessing the evidence before implementing new ideas or changing one's practices.
- Students – undergraduate, postgraduate, or those studying for practical doctorate courses – who wish to carry out research as part of accredited courses. Some of the projects within this context could, of course, belong to the first category where a university course may provide added support to the action researcher.

I hope that both the above groups will find the step-by-step guidance provided in this book useful.

My own belief is that carrying out action research is all about developing the act of knowing through observation, listening, analysing, questioning, and being involved in constructing one's own knowledge. The new knowledge and experiences, gained will inform the researcher's future direction and influence action.

This book is written in an interactive style and the reader is invited to join the author in exploring aspects of what is involved in conducting *practitioner research*, as it is sometimes called. The use of examples, case studies and short tasks in the book should make the contents more accessible.

The book is presented in eight chapters. *Chapter 1* explores the concept of action research and considers how it is distinctive from other forms of research. Readers are provided with an overview of how action research has developed over the past decades, its background and the key concepts of action research – planning action, evaluation, refinement, reflection, theory building. References to experts' views and models of action research should assist the new action researcher to plan his or her work as well as help to justify the choice. The possible advantages of using action research as a methodology are discussed here. Detailed examples of action research projects, carried out by practitioners from a variety of contexts and dealing with a range of topics, are also presented. The chapter concludes with a discussion of the theoretical underpinnings of action research in order to support the researcher to articulate his or her positioning in terms of ontological and epistemological assumptions.

Chapters 2 to 6 will address the various stages of action research. *Chapter 2* addresses some of the criticisms raised against action research as a methodology. It explores the views of experts – in terms of its role in the professional development of a researcher – and discusses the structure and processes involved in conducting action research. The aim of this chapter is to offer practical guidelines to action researchers who are about to take the first step. It offers examples of topics selected by practitioners for action research. Although the stages of action research are not strictly linear, it should help a researcher to think in terms of planning the project in stages – with a built-in flexibility to refine, make adjustments, and change direction within the structure. This feature of flexibility for refinement makes action research an eminently suitable method of enquiry for practitioners. Using examples, the reader is guided in his or her choice of topic for research and is also helped to consider the suitability of using action research in various contexts.

Chapter 3 focuses on the role of a literature search and writing research reviews within action research. The justification for undertaking research reviews and guidance on how to gather, organize, analyse and make use of what is read are presented. Utilising electronic sources for a literature search is dealt with in this chapter, along with some additional support culled from the evaluation of sources of literature obtained from the Internet.

Having selected a topic and collected the background literature, a researcher would then begin to plan his or her project. *Chapter 4* supports the reader, using practical examples to illustrate how interventions and activities have been planned by other practitioners. In my experience, one of the most challenging aspects of conducting action research arises when making decisions on what kind of data are needed and how to collect these to achieve the aims of the project. The process of action planning is discussed and a practical planning sheet is also provided. Special consideration is given at this point to the all-important aspect of 'when things go wrong' as researchers are conducting research. In *Chapter 5*, different types of instrumentation for gathering data are presented. Using practical illustrations, the advantages and disadvantages of using different methods are discussed. The importance of being systematic in the data-gathering process is emphasized. Ethical considerations are also dealt with.

Chapter 6 focuses on the complex issue of the analysis of data and data display. Action research, by its nature, is unlikely to produce universally generalisable findings – its purpose is to generate principles based on experience. The analysis within action research seeks to identify themes and issues which are relevant and applicable to a particular situation. Guidance is provided on how the data may be analysed and presented, including the use of computer software packages. Examples of practitioners' accounts of data analysis are provided within the chapter. The chapter concludes with a consideration of the fundamental issues of establishing the trustworthiness of evidence and the validity of both the procedures and the conclusions.

The type of report written by an action researcher will depend on the circumstances of that researcher. Funded research requires a certain format to be followed, whereas a report in the form of a dissertation for an accredited course will need to follow a different and often predetermined format. Examples of producing reports and the processes involved in writing up or disseminating findings are provided in *Chapter 7* and *Chapter 8* discusses more ways of disseminating the findings. Guidance on how to publish action research in various forms – newsletters, conference presentations and journal articles – is also provided.

There is a reference section in the final part of the book which draws on a range of authors who have contributed to the ongoing dialogue on action research. Further readings and a list of useful websites are included at the end of the chapters where these are appropriate.

What I have attempted to do in this book is to provide a clear set of practical guidelines for undertaking action research. I hope you will find them useful. Working alongside action researchers in various settings has provided me with a great deal of enjoyment and satisfaction over the past years. I hope you will share some of what I have experienced through your reading of this book.

1

What is action research?

This chapter focuses on:

- the nature of action research;
- the development of action research;
- what is involved in action research;
- models and definitions of action research proposed by experts in the field;
- examples of action research carried out by a range of practitioners;
- the theoretical underpinnings of action research.

Research is a form of disciplined enquiry leading to the generation of knowledge. The knowledge that your research generates is derived from a range of approaches. Your approach to research may vary according to the context of your study, your beliefs, the strategies you employ, and the methods you use. The paradigm (a collection of assumptions and beliefs which guide you along the path to conducting research and interpreting findings) you select will be guided by your subject discipline and beliefs. Action research is a specific method of conducting research by professionals and practitioners with the ultimate aim of improving practice. Throughout this book, where it is appropriate, references are made as to how epistemological and ontological views may influence your research and the research methods you use. Further readings are also provided at the end of the chapter for those who wish to delve deeper into these issues.

What is the purpose of conducting action research? In the context of this book, action research supports practitioners to seek ways in which they can provide good quality education by transforming the quality of teaching-related activities, thereby enhancing students' learning. With this purpose in mind the following features of the methodology of action research are worthy of consideration:

- Action research is a method used for improving educational practice. It involves action, evaluation and reflection and, based on gathered evidence, changes in practice are implemented.
- Action research is participative and collaborative; it is undertaken by individuals, with a common purpose.

- It is situation-based.
- It develops reflection based on the interpretations made by participants.
- Knowledge is created through action, and at the point of application.
- Action research can involve problem-solving, if the solution to the problem leads to the improvement of practice.
- In action research findings emerge as action develops, but they are not conclusive or absolute.

The following extract, included by Reason and Bradbury (2001: 1) in the introduction to their *Handbook of Action Research*, is helpful to us in trying to locate action research as a unique paradigm:

> For me it is really a quest for life, to understand life and to create what I call living knowledge – knowledge which is valid for the people with whom I work and for myself.
>
> (Marja Liisa Swantz)

So, what is this living knowledge? As the above authors explain, the purpose of action research is to produce practical knowledge that is useful to people in the everyday conduct of their lives and to see that action research is about working towards practical outcomes, and also about

> creating new forms of understanding, since action without reflection and understanding is blind, just as theory without action is meaningless. The participatory nature of action research/makes it only possible *with*, *for* and *by* persons and communities, ideally involving all stakeholders both in the questioning and sense making that informs the research, and in the action which is its focus.
>
> (Reason and Bradbury, 2001: 2)

During my first meetings with teachers and trainee teachers who are about to undertake action research, I share with them a strong belief that I hold. And here it is. I believe that ultimately the quality of educational experiences provided to children will depend on the ability of a teacher to stand back, question and reflect on his or her practice, and continually strive to make the necessary changes. This is true of any practitioner. These processes of reflection and self-evaluation do not happen by accident and I believe that carrying out action research provides practitioners with an opportunity to be engaged in such processes in a meaningful way. With the above statements in mind, I define action research as an enquiry, undertaken with rigour and understanding so as to constantly refine practice; the emerging evidence-based outcomes will then contribute to the researching practitioner's continuing professional development.

   In this chapter I will trace the development of action research as a methodology over the past few decades and then consider the different perspectives and models provided by experts in the field. Different models of action research are explored and an attempt is made to identify the unique features of action research which should make it an attractive mode of research for practitioners. An understanding of different interpretations and viewpoints of action research should be useful to readers whether they are about to start a project or are in the process of doing one. Researchers who are carrying out action research as part of an accredited course are usually expected to demonstrate their understanding of the processes involved. Those who are involved in action research following personal interests, or as part of their institutional change, will also need to gain insights into the processes involved, so that they can engage in action research with greater confidence and understanding. Examples of action research projects undertaken by practitioners in a range of situations are provided. In the final section of this chapter, we examine the philosophies and theoretical underpinnings relating to action research.

The development of action research: a brief background

Whether you are a novice or progressing with an action research project, it would be useful for you to be aware of how action research developed as a method for carrying out research over the past few decades. Zeichner (2001) and Hopkins (2002) provide us with an overview of how action research developed as a research tradition. The work of Kurt Lewin (1946), who researched into social issues, is often described as a major landmark in the development of action research as a methodology. Lewin's work was followed by that of Stephen Corey and others in the USA, who applied this methodology for researching into educational issues.

In Britain, according to Hopkins (2002), the origins of action research can be traced back to the Schools Council's Humanities Curriculum Project (1967–72) with its emphasis on an experimental curriculum and the reconceptualization of curriculum development. Following on this project, Elliot and Adelman (1976) used action research in their Teaching Project when examining classroom practice.

The most well-known proponent of action research in the UK has been Lawrence Stenhouse whose seminal (1975) work, *An Introduction to Curriculum Research and Development*, added to the appeal of action research for studying the theory and practice of teaching and the curriculum. For Stenhouse (1983), action research was about emancipation and intellectual, moral and spiritual autonomy. There was also the participatory research movement supported by Stephen Kemmis and Robert McTaggart, as reported by Hopkins (2002), at Deakin University in Australia.

In the past two decades action research has been growing in popularity in the United States where it has often been supported by universities. Zeichner

(2001) points out that most of the action research carried out in the past involved university academics and teachers and represented the rejection of a standards- or objective-based approach to curriculum development, in favour of one that was based on a pedagogy-driven conception of curriculum change as a process dependent on teachers' capacities for reflection. According to this view, Zeichner maintains, the act of curriculum theorizing is not so much the application of classroom theory learned in the university as it is the generation of theory from attempts to change curriculum practice in schools.

In the past decade there has been growing interest in action research as a methodology across the world. Educationists in different roles – teachers, policy makers and administrators – see the potential of action research in producing applied knowledge in a number of applied contexts which can be of practical use. An increasing number of papers based on practitioner research are being presented at international research conferences. There are several websites and practical networks, such as CARN (see the websites mentioned at the end of this chapter) which provide forums for those interested in action research as a methodology, as well as the existence of international journals, such as *Educational Action Research* (once again, see the relevant website at the end of this chapter).

What is involved in action research?

Research is about generating knowledge. Action research creates knowledge based on enquiries conducted within specific and often practical contexts. As articulated earlier, the purpose of action research is to learn through action leading to personal or professional development. It is participatory in nature which led Kemmis and McTaggart (2000: 595) to describe it as *participatory research*. These authors maintain that action research involves a spiral of self-contained cycles of:

- planning a change;
- acting and observing the process and consequences of the change;
- reflecting on these processes and consequences and then replanning;
- acting and observing;
- reflecting;
- and so on ...

Figure 1.1 illustrates this spiral model of action research proposed by Kemmis and McTaggart, although the authors advise us against using this as a rigid structure. They maintain that in reality the process may not be as neat as the spiral suggests. The stages defined above, they maintain, *overlap*, and initial plans quickly become obsolete in the light of learning from experience. *In reality the process is likely to be more fluid, open and responsive.*

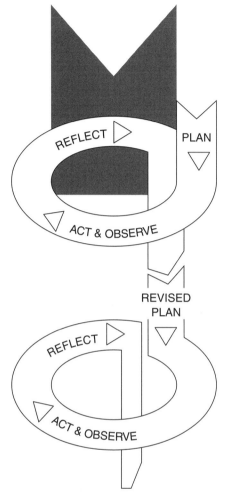

Figure 1.1   The action research spiral

I find the spiral model appealing because it offers the opportunity to visit a phenomenon at a higher level each time, and thus to progress towards greater overall understanding. By carrying out action research using this model, one can understand a particular issue within an educational context and make informed decisions through enhanced understanding. It is fundamentally about empowerment.

Several other models have also been put forward by those who have studied different aspects of action research and I will present some of these here. My purpose in so doing is to enable you as the reader to analyse the principles involved in these models which should, in turn, lead to a deeper understanding of the processes involved in action research. No single model is being recommended and, as you may notice, they do have many similarities. An action researcher should adopt the models which suit his or her purpose most or adapt them to fit that purpose.

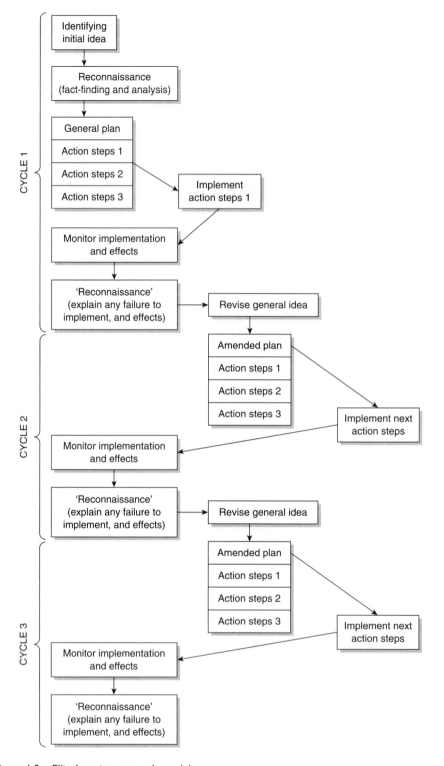

Figure 1.2   Elliot's action research model

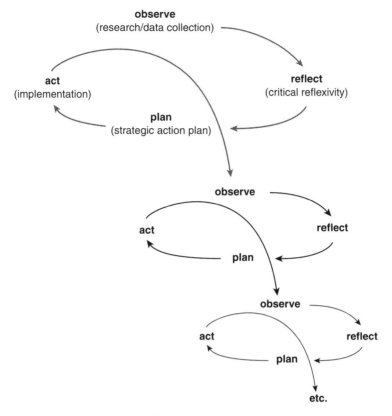

Figure 1.3   O'Leary's cycles of research

The model suggested by Elliot (1991: 71) includes reconnaissance – namely fact-finding and analysis – within each stage of the action research, as can be seen in Figure 1.2. Other models, such as O'Leary's (2004: 141) cycles of action research shown in Figure 1.3, portray action research as a cyclic process which takes shape as knowledge emerges. In O'Leary's model, it is stressed that 'cycles converge towards better situation understanding and improved action implementation; and are based in evaluative practice that alters between action and critical reflection' (2004: 140). The author sees action research as an experiential learning approach to change the goal of which is to continually refine the methods, data and interpretation in the light of the understanding developed in the earlier cycles. And finally, in Macintyre's (2000: 1) representation of the stages in action research, the processes involved are signposted as shown in Figure 1.4.

Although it is useful to consider different models, I need to include a word of caution here. Excessive reliance on a particular model, or following the stages or cycles of a particular model too rigidly, could adversely affect the unique opportunity offered by the emerging nature and flexibility which are the hallmarks of action research. Models of practice presented in this chapter are not intended to offer straitjackets to fit an enquiry. It would be useful for you to construct your own model describing the particular paths of the enquiry you will be making.

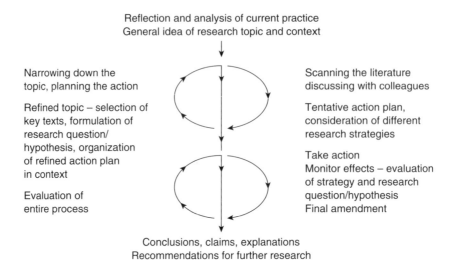

Reflection and analysis of current practice
General idea of research topic and context

Narrowing down the
topic, planning the action

Refined topic – selection of
key texts, formulation of
research question/
hypothesis, organization
of refined action plan
in context

Evaluation of
entire process

Scanning the literature
discussing with colleagues

Tentative action plan,
consideration of different
research strategies

Take action
Monitor effects – evaluation
of strategy and research
question/hypothesis
Final amendment

Conclusions, claims, explanations
Recommendations for further research

Figure 1.4   An action research cycle

Some definitions of action research

At this point, I feel it may be useful to explore some of the definitions and observations on action research as a methodology offered by different authors. Bassey (1998: 93) describes 'action research as an enquiry which is carried out in order to understand, to evaluate and then to change, in order to improve educational practice'. Hopkins (2002: 41) maintains that 'action research combines a substantive act with a research procedure; it is action disciplined by enquiry, a personal attempt at understanding while engaged in a process of improvement and reform'. Cohen and Manion (1994: 192) describe the emergent nature of action research in their definition. They explain action research as

> essentially an on-the-spot procedure designed to deal with a concrete problem located in an immediate situation. This means that ideally, the step-by-step process is constantly monitored over varying periods of time and by a variety of mechanisms (questionnaires, diaries, interviews and case studies, for example) so that the ensuing feedback may be translated into modifications, adjustment, directional changes, redefinitions, as necessary, so as to bring about lasting benefit to the ongoing process itself rather than to some future occasion.

Bell (1999) comments on the practical, problem-solving nature of action research which she believes makes this approach attractive to practitioner-researchers. She also highlights the fact that action research is directed towards greater understanding and the improvement of practice over a period of time.

A careful study of the definitions and viewpoints I have presented in this section should help us to highlight some unique features of action research.

The key words include *better understanding, improvement, reform, problem-solving, step-by-step process* and *modification.* These words also perhaps demonstrate the reasons for the popularity of action research as a mode of study for practitioners.

Much of the literature on action research emphasizes the practical nature of this type of research. It deals with the practices of various people, quite often within their settings. Its main purpose is to improve practice – either one's own practice or the effectiveness of an institution. I consider action research as a constructive enquiry, during which the researcher constructs his or her knowledge of specific issues through planning, acting, evaluating, refining and learning from the experience. It is a continuous learning process in which the researcher learns and also shares the newly generated knowledge with those who may benefit from it.

Examples of action research projects

In the next section, I have included some examples of action research projects carried out by practitioners in a number of settings. They are deliberately kept brief and only used as examples. As you read these examples, as told by the researchers themselves in a summary form and style selected by them, try to consider how their experiences relate to the different models and definitions presented earlier in this chapter. You may ask yourself whether these examples have elements in common with your own situation and needs.

Example

Introducing the principles of 'Assessment for Learning' in my class (Christine, a teacher)

Context and background

I teach 10 year olds in an inner city school. I am keen to keep up-to-date with developments in education. It was a talk on assessment which I attended at the local teachers' centre that provided the spark for what was to become a year-long action research project. I have responsibility for assessment in my school and, for some time, I was feeling uneasy about the closed nature of the assessment procedures we used. I could not articulate what I wished to change, but after the speaker told us about a study by Black and William on 'Assessment for Learning' (1998) I felt I could do something about changing things.

'Assessment for Learning' emphasizes the importance of formative assessment in enhancing children's learning. The speaker talked about some research carried out by the above authors which suggests that if teachers involved children in their own assessment it would lead to higher attainment. After the talk, I thought about it and

(Continued)

(Continued)

wondered why formative assessment is so powerful and came up with two possible reasons for that. One must be the increased motivation of the students as a result of continuous feedback; the other is the effect it has on more powerful 'personalized learning' through their involvement in the process of learning and assessment. Then it dawned on me that I could undertake a study as part of a practical project for a Master's module on 'Teaching and Learning' which I was studying at the local university. I had not heard of action research before I started.

What did I do?

The first step
The first step was to take a good look at what was happening in our school. Children had regular class tests in mathematics and spellings; their work was marked and graded and all the children took standardized tests at the end of every year. My colleagues at the university, who were also registered for a module in action research, suggested that I keep diary entries of my journey through the project as it would help me not only to make modifications to my actions but also when writing up the project. As I reflected on what was happening, I recorded '*A world full of tests, to what end?*' as my first reaction. Now I had to consider what I wanted to do. Introducing self-assessment as part of everyday learning seemed a good starting point. This was the more challenging part. I felt both excited and nervous.

At the beginning, I was not sure how I was going to conduct a study. Soon I realized I had to ask myself some questions. What was I going to do? What was the purpose? What did I expect to get from the study? Who is going to be involved in the study? What did it entail? Could I approach my colleagues who teach parallel classes to be involved? The last question was particularly challenging as it caused me some anxiety as to whether there would be opposition from my colleagues who may have perceived my ideas as adding to their workload. Finally, I decided to study the outcomes of my ideas with my class and just another class teacher of 10 year olds, with whom I worked closely anyway. She was pleased that I had asked her to be a research partner.

My colleague Alison and I made an initial plan for the study. We listed a sequence of activities such as reading Black and William's paper outlining the benefits of self-assessment and listing the benefits. We drew up a schedule to take a close look at what involvement, if any, pupils had in their own assessment at the start of the project. We were horrified by what we found. There was hardly any stage in the day where we asked children to comment on what they had learnt or how, or even how they thought they had done. Assessment in our school seemed to be a mechanical exercise of ticks, grades and marks.

(Continued)

(Continued)

Moving on

The next step was deciding what to do. We decided to introduce three activities based on our readings. The first was to make children more aware of what the learning intentions of a lesson were. This, we felt, would focus children's learning so they would be more aware of what they were expected to learn and hence would take more responsibility for their learning. The second was to introduce a weekly diary in which children recorded what they had learnt and how they thought they had learnt and understood new ideas. Another change involved following up what had been said at the session at the teachers' centre; instead of giving a grade for a piece of work, we decided to write a comment. The third activity was to organize a time at the end of the week to discuss, with the children, the best lessons in the week and let children speak freely about why they thought some lessons had been better than others.

Monitoring progress

We knew we needed to monitor what happened with each of the activities. We felt we needed to be realistic and select the kind of data we could manage both in terms of data gathering and analysis. With this in mind, we decided to establish a baseline first.

   At the end of two lessons, we asked children what they thought they were supposed to have learnt and to write down their responses. We also kept notes on what they thought they had learnt from the two lessons. And, finally, we wrote a comment underneath the marks awarded for a piece of work and asked the children afterwards what they thought of the comments. While analysing the data we found out that in spite of sharing the learning outcomes with the children they had not taken much notice of these and could not articulate what these were. For the second part, when asked what they had learnt, the responses ranged from two- or three-line vague scribbles to 'don't knows', to one case of 'nothing really', and 'I already knew what she [the teacher] was going to teach anyway'. The third set of data was the most revealing. Most of the children had taken note of their marks and could tell us what these were as well as those for some of their friends also. But they had not read our comments. This was not surprising to us, as I had read about this tendency in the literature.

Revising the plans

The intervention activities we had planned were revised in light of our observations. We decided to photocopy the learning intentions and give copies to the children to stick in their notebooks, so that they would constantly be aware of what they were expected to learn. The second intervention – keeping a learning diary – was found

(Continued)

(Continued)

difficult by most children as they were not used to reflecting on their learning. The initial idea of keeping a general learning diary for all subjects was abandoned as impractical and we concentrated on mathematics lessons only. The third change was to award marks only for some pieces of work and to write a set of comments for the others.

What happened?

The project lasted for two terms. We collected evidence of what was happening by discussions between us, through reading our own diaries of significant events and by making our interpretations of them. Evidence of children being able to articulate their learning intentions and to take note of their teacher's comments in workbooks was generated. What we found out from the project outcomes was very useful to us and there was also enough evidence for us to see that our activities had yielded some success in achieving more involvement of children with the assessment of their learning.

We were aware that what we had done and found out were useful only to us initially, but during a staff meeting we shared our project with the whole staff and teaching assistants who were very interested in our findings. At a later stage we gave a presentation to our cluster of neighbouring schools; the participants were interested especially because we were drawing on practical activities and highlighting what could be achieved within our classes. Of course, I also wrote a report of what we did for my course assignment.

What did I learn from this project?

Although the project only lasted six months, the level of my personal engagement was high. Before and during the project I had read about the action research cycle I could use for the project; but in reality the cycle had to be broken many times when things didn't go according to plan. Even small things, such as delays in getting replies from parents giving permission for the children to take part in the project, created difficulties. Sharing our findings, as they emerged, with the head teacher and other colleagues also caused some anxiety. The children were very enthusiastic about the project (as part of the ethical procedure, we had also asked them if they were happy for us to collect their work and discuss them with others). The outcomes of the project may have been influenced by the children's initial keenness; we decided to keep a watch on this after the project had concluded. One of the features of practitioner research in their own setting is that the personal learning continues long after the formal work is concluded.

I believe my questioning and analytical skills improved as a result of carrying out an action research project. Throughout the project, my research partner and myself constantly asked ourselves: 'What is happening here?' Through such questioning, interpreting what happened in the classroom and reflection I know that my practice has improved. The process of sharing my project with colleagues also enhanced my professional confidence.

Example

Responding to the needs of mature students enrolling for teacher training courses (Lisa, a lecturer in higher education)

Context and background

I believe in the principle of lifelong learning. I feel it is important that we encourage mature students who have worked, or have spent a number of years doing other things, to join teacher-training courses and complete them. These situations include women who may have had a break in their career to bring up families and those who have followed other careers and now wish to become teachers later in life. A third group consists of people who have not had the opportunity to obtain a degree when they left school, but have instead followed other methods of study to get a qualification to prepare them to enroll for a teacher-training course. The beginning of the project I am about to describe can be traced back to an after-lecture conversation I had with a group of mature teacher trainees in my university who told me that before they joined the course they had felt anxious about joining the course and studying with younger members. They also told me that they still felt anxious during sessions and were worried that their lack of confidence could affect their teaching during their initial placements in schools. A group of my colleagues, who felt the same way as I did, were keen to develop methods to encourage these students and provide a positive learning environment for them. With this mind, we set up an action research project with support funding from staff research funds at the university. We started with a small questionnaire survey to explore how mature students felt as members of the course. The responses suggested that a significant number of mature students felt uneasy about returning to study. They felt anxious in the company of younger students, who they thought had better skills with technology and writing essays and appeared more confident. They also felt uneasy about participating in discussions and having a general lack of confidence. The next step was to plan an intervention. We believed that our contribution to knowledge would be two-fold. First, we would develop a set of strategies which would help our mature students and these would also be useful to other practitioners in similar situations. Second, the general lessons learnt from our project could be shared with those who have responsibility for encouraging the widening participation of adult learners in higher education.

Preparation and planning

The team read all the available literature, obtained through our manual and web-search, and highlighted those aspects that had been identified as barriers to mature students who shied away from joining universities to acquire qualifications,

(Continued)

(Continued)

with special attention given to teacher-trainees. Some of the aspects which were identified in our own previous survey with our students, as reasons for causing anxiety among mature students, were also highlighted in other literature. We made a summary of these. We selected an action research approach, as we felt it would enable the teaching team to be part of the process of change at both stages – both for the identification of what needed to be done and for the implementation of strategies in response to these. We decided to work closely with the students after explaining the purpose of the project to them and the response was overwhelmingly positive. We took note of the features of action research which made it a suitable method for our project. The project was located within our working context and it provided us with opportunities for collaborating with our students. The emerging nature of the interpretations and findings made it necessary to use iterative cycles in our model of action research.

What did we do?

Although it is not possible here to describe fully what we did during a one-year project, I will include what we felt were the most useful parts of the project. Our first cycle of action was designed to find out, in detail, the experiences and views of both the lecturers and students. Data collection included finding out the total numbers of mature students enrolled on our courses, their backgrounds as written on their initial application forms and their gender distribution to look for possible trends. Both individual and group interviews were carried out with the mature students and the data were analysed and compared with the perceptions of the tutors. We found a good match in the two sets of data. In order to validate the evidence generated a group of tutors who were not involved in teaching the students in our project at that time were recruited, as Critical Friends, to read through transcripts, notes of our meetings and our needs-analysis of what action was required. Students were asked to comment on all the interventions which were designed to address the needs – such as small group discussions where mature students worked with other students, extra ICT sessions, having specialist tutors to support them with structuring assignments, peer group marking and reading drafts of their work. We had found that many of the mature students were fearful of all forms of assessment. They felt they lacked both study skills and the skills required read to academic papers. Many of them felt insecure and anxious about participating in group discussions. Other areas identified by many as requiring support were information technology skills together with skills of time management.

(Continued)

(Continued)

What did I learn from the project?

The collaborative learning experience was very rewarding. The knowledge we created was based on the collaborative effort of all the participants – lecturers and students. Interventions were informed by the on-going data gathering. For us – the tutors – it was an opportunity to stand back and reflect, whilst addressing a real problem within a real context. Action research provided a methodology which enabled us to make revisions to our plans and to respond to needs as they arose while at the same time maintaining rigour in the quality of data collection, analysis and interpretation. Our dissemination took the form of published descriptive case studies which captured the reality of the situations; these made a contribution to the literature on widening participation and lifelong learning.

How did the action cycles work?

The first cycle
   Our concern was raised
   Research question was set up: How can we improve provision for mature students joining our teacher training course?
   Explored views and problems through questionnaires, surveys, interviews, existing literature and discussions
   Analysed the data and reflected on the initial findings
   Shared the findings and discussed these with students and tutors
   Validated the data and findings with critical friends
   Carried out a needs analysis

Second cycle – organize action
   Design activities: for example, IT sessions, small discussion groups, assignment support, mature students sharing their skills – from previous employment and experience – with new students
   Set up structures for students and tutors to evaluate activities
   Second set of interviews
   Validation meeting
   Wrote up interim report including suggestions for changes

Third cycle – further planning
   Refined actions
   Prepared the internal evaluation of methods and findings
   Presented this to colleagues
   Newsletter on website
   National dissemination – two conferences and two published papers

Example

Christine – a teacher working within a national network of action researchers

Background

It all started when, as part of the government's initiative to enhance provision for gifted and talented students, the Department for Education and Skills in the UK invited proposals for funding to be awarded to individual schools or groups of practitioners to carry out action research into aspects of nurturing talents in younger children – specifically children aged 4–7. Brunel University tutors, who had carried out a number of studies into early giftedness and its development, were invited to guide the action researchers. The purpose of commissioning the project was to generate a knowledge base in gifted education with a particular emphasis on children within the first years of schooling. Fourteen groups of practitioners (across the country) were awarded funding to carry out action research into selected topics. The project provided an opportunity for a group of researchers to work with university academics to explore the best ways of developing talent in younger children. One of the requirements for providing funding was that the action researchers had to produce case studies of their project and that their findings would be published on the government website. Researchers were also invited to present at national conferences.

My context

In response to the invitation to participate in a set of projects, our local district adviser (Joy) applied for funding to set up a 'pull out' group of exceptionally able pupils whose educational needs, we felt, were not being met within their schools. Schools usually have only one or two of the type of child we had in mind and, within a busy classroom, teachers did not always have the time to devote to them. Some of the children who had been referred to the gifted and talented adviser, Joy, had been showing disruptive behaviour and she felt this may have been due to their frustration caused by having to work on tasks which were cognitively undemanding. Following a successful application for funding, Joy invited me to set up an enrichment cluster. Initially I was nervous when I was told we had to attend some sessions at the university, as my track record of higher education was not all that successful.

Meeting others who were also conducting action research was very useful. The fact that the project was funded by external sources and its findings had to be shared with others across the country caused some anxiety, but it also highlighted the importance of having a robust structure and set of outcomes. During the university sessions we discussed action research as a methodology for generating principles based on practice and were reassured by the flexibility it allows.

(Continued)

(Continued)

Outcomes

The first challenge was to identify a focus and decide on what we were hoping to achieve. The outcomes would be useful to colleagues within my own education authority and they should also be of interest to colleagues who may have read my case study and listened to my story. Right from the start, I had to remind myself, reinforced by the university staff, that the purpose of the research was not just to help a group of children but also to extract principles and models from the project which could be useful to other practitioners.

A group of 20 children, aged 5–6, were selected by their class teachers from a number of schools and sent to the enrichment class run by myself and two assistants from a local school. The group attended a programme of enrichment activities once a week – on Thursday afternoons. The first challenge was to establish a system for the selection of the pupils and this was not easy. My own feeling was that teachers' close observation of children's achievement or potential would be a good starting point. One could always revise this. As it happened, the children who were selected also scored high on a standardized test that we used, suggesting that teachers' judgements were quite accurate.

As it was a new area of exploration for me, I read some research papers on Renzulli's [an expert on enrichment work in schools] enrichment activities which are very popular in the USA. I also received guidance from the tutors at the university on setting up enrichment activities. In addition, I conducted a web search for other related literature.

A set of activities was planned, taking into account the context of the children's backgrounds and the Early Years policy of the local education district. A local university was involved in providing expertise in some areas of advanced concepts. The project was running smoothly when, during our second meeting, the whole question of how we could evaluate the project came up. This part was quite demanding for me and I needed guidance. The first set of questionnaires I designed for parents and teachers needed substantial revision. Triangulation was achieved by seeking perspectives from the various persons involved in the project. Photographs were taken and some children were interviewed before, during and at the conclusion of the project. Teachers' views were also gathered.

What did I learn?

Our action research project was disseminated at national conferences as papers and displays were organized at exhibitions of 'best practices' in education. Project findings were shared with colleagues in the local teachers' professional development centre. In this project the university researchers worked with practitioners co-creating knowledge. Case studies and research papers were written and

(Continued)

(Continued)

published. The dissemination of the processes we adopted for the action research projects and the outcomes of the project have added to the knowledge base of nurturing talent in the early years of schooling, which is an area where very little research has been done internationally. It was a valuable professional development exercise for me. The personal theories I have constructed during the project have enhanced my confidence and I no longer feel that research is something which is done *on* children and teachers by academics, but that it can be done *by teachers.*

My personal learning includes the development of systematic work and higher order questioning, analysing data and generating evidence. I have also become aware of the benefits of belonging to a collaborative network of action researchers who have contributed to my professional and personal knowledge. I learnt that the anxiety I felt during different stages of the project and the temptation to give up are part of the action research process.

Example

Julian – class teacher of 8 year old children

Background

Like most people in my profession, I was excited when a national initiative for improving mathematics teaching was introduced. The training which was organized and the documentation accompanying the initiative recommended a three-part structure for the daily mathematics lesson: start with mental mathematics, follow with the main lesson, and then a 'conclusion' session with a discussion of what children had learnt and how they had learnt, which was to last for about ten minutes. I was broadly happy with this structure at first, but later I became unhappy about my 'conclusion' sessions. Those sessions seemed to be unproductive because my children did not actively participate in this part of the lesson. I studied the main purpose of the 'conclusion' part in the documentation; it was to assess children's level of understanding of what had been taught, rectify any misconceptions, help them to make connections with previously taught ideas and highlight what progress had been made. I believe in the 'constructivist' philosophy of learning where children actively construct their own learning. A discussion with children on how they learn mathematics is well within my philosophy of learning and teaching. So why didn't it work? How could I improve the session?

What was the problem?

It was clear that I was not meeting the objectives of the concluding part of my maths lesson, as my children were not actively participating in the discussion. Either they

(Continued)

(Continued)

provided one-word answers to my questions or just kept quiet. At first I was not sure how I would encourage children to participate in the discussion which is integral to this part of the lesson. I was unhappy about the problem, but did not really know how to solve it.

An opportunity

I felt that an opportunity had arisen here; I could choose this topic for investigation in my MA dissertation. Action research, or participatory research, would enable me to work flexibly without a tight and pre-determined structure. It would also allow me the freedom to plan, act, evaluate and reflect on my ideas before putting them into practice. As I was embarking on the action research project for the purpose of accreditation for a Master's degree, I knew I had to follow some academic guidelines. I had to undertake a review of the literature relating to the teaching and learning of mathematics. I also had to demonstrate my understanding of action research and justify why I had chosen it as a method to conduct my research.

My research question was: How can I make the children in my class take a more active part in the 'conclusion' of a lesson, discussing what they had learnt and how? Working with my own class to explore strategies made the planning easier. I still had to have a sharp focus on what I wanted to achieve. It took about four weeks of reading and discussion, both with colleagues and the local mathematics adviser, before I finally made a firm plan. At the planning stage, I needed to set out my aims and objectives. Why was I doing this? What made me want to research into this topic? What evidence should I present in justifying the need to carry out this piece of research?

What did I do?

As it was a new initiative, no evaluative literature was available for me to read. So I had to justify why I thought there was a problem with the concluding part of my lesson by using my own observations. However, I used literature I had found on 'teaching and learning' to assess the effectiveness of the sessions in terms of students' motivation and interest; clearly these were missing from my lessons. I constructed a 'To do' list.

- Refer to the objectives of the three-part lesson in the documentation provided in the government policy document, especially with reference to the discussion in the concluding part of the lesson, which is expected to take place.
- Collect information about how the objectives are being met in my sessions. Are my concerns borne out by the data?
- Analyse my concerns.
- Plan strategies to encourage active participation. Look at what mathematics educators have suggested as strategies to promote discussion in mathematics lessons and construct a work plan.

(Continued)

(Continued)

- Implement the plan.
- Gather data through observations and a personal diary of any changes in children's attitudes and responses.
- Analyse the data for any changes and indicators of an enhanced understanding of concepts involved in the main lesson (make changes as necessary).
- Evaluate the effectiveness of my intervention strategies.

I implemented a set of strategies for increasing student participation. One was to reduce the number of closed questions which elicited short and vague answers. By asking open-ended questions and using probing techniques, students' responses became more full and their enthusiasm was greater. Another strategy I used was to give students a set of questions (earlier in the lesson, while they were working on tasks) which were to be discussed in the concluding session so that they had time to think about their own learning which, in turn, provided them with more opportunities to plan what to discuss. I implemented these strategies in every lesson for three months and collected a good deal of useful data which I analysed and evaluated against my objectives.

The final step

As part of the writing-up for my dissertation, I discussed my findings in relation to the aims and objectives for the study. I justified the selection of action research as a method in terms of its flexibility and the opportunities it affords for locating the fieldwork in one's professional context. I found the methodology of action research highly suitable for my purpose. I was able to work on a topic of personal interest which was also part of my professional context. The structure allowed me to refine my strategies and directions as I progressed through the project. My personal learning and the influence the study had had on my practice were highlighted, as well as an acknowledgement of any shortcomings. The ways in which my findings could be useful to other practitioners were also stated.

Action research and its theoretical underpinnings

Several of the salient features of action research have been exemplified through the use of case studies in the previous section. The context of all the enquiries – the education system – may vary. And yet, always for the one or more action researchers involved, the ultimate objective of the research enquiry was the production of greater understanding of the selected groups within the education system, so as to produce practical principles and strategies for the improvement of that system. A possible common denominator of action research enquiries is the population of participants – children, teachers and other adults who work within the education system – engaged in a collaboration designed to benefit all of those involved.

The life courses of all of those who are part of the research process are enhanced. That enhancement may be explained with reference to two elements: a greater understanding of the role of the participants in the education system founded on more detailed and profound knowledge and a greater understanding of the self, due to informed negotiated meanings of activities shared with others and a developed capacity for construction and analysis.

To gain a somewhat global perspective of what constitutes action research, primary consideration must be given to the fact that it involves a social system – consisting of interacting humans – and not a physical system comprised of inert or inanimate objects. To supplement the following discussion on the theoretical underpinnings, I have included explanations of the terminology used in the glossary at the end of this book.

The quest for knowledge and understanding has a long history. Metaphysics launched the quest by analysing human experience of the environment so as to distinguish between knowledge of an immutable reality and the observed visible projection of that reality. The search for knowledge, the epistemological pursuit, created a hierarchy with knowledge of an immutable reality regarded as superior to the acquaintance with things humans could sense without the aid of artificial instruments.

For social systems a postmodernist approach seeks knowledge within a social system as opposed to the positivist approach which demands logical or scientific support for beliefs. Action research does not subscribe to a positivist viewpoint concerning evidence and conclusions inherent in a research exercise. It supports a postmodernist attitude to epistemology (theory of knowledge) – advocating questions and discussions within the research exercise – so that emerging beliefs, whilst not embedded in an immutable reality, are the product of a negotiated consensus contributing to the future harmony of the actions and elevations of life courses.

Conceptualizing action research

Research is concerned with the generation of knowledge. By carrying out action research practitioners are involved in exploring ways of improving their practice and the knowledge created is often context-specific. In this section we take a close look at the theoretical underpinnings of action research. In order to *conceptualize* action research, let us make a start with a consideration of what Levin and Greenwood (2001: 105) have to say.

- That action research is context bound and addresses real life problems.
- That action research is an enquiry where participants and researchers co-generate knowledge through collaborative communicative processes in which all participants' contributions are taken seriously.
- That the meanings constructed in the enquiry process lead to social action or these reflections and action lead to the construction of new meanings.

- That the credibility/validity of action research knowledge is measured according to whether the actions that arise from it solve problems (workability) and increase participants' control over their own situation.

As an action researcher the new knowledge you generate and the personal theories you develop will be based on your experiences. These theories are important to you and will impact on those working with you in your institution or community of researchers. During an interesting session I had with students studying for doctoral programmes at our university, we focused on the need for a researcher to articulate his or her theoretical stance or philosophical positioning whichever methodology they chose to select. During these discussions, students who intended to use action research as their methodology (following a plan-act-evaluate-reflect cycle) placed action research within a *constructivist* methodology as they felt they were constructing their own meanings and understandings throughout the period of the research and that these constructions would continue after their enquiry had been completed.

Action researchers constructing their own knowledge

So what is constructivism? According to von Glasersfeld (1987), there are important principles on which constructivism is based. First, knowledge is not passively received but actively built up by the cognising subject; and secondly, the function of cognition is adaptive and serves the organization of the experimental world, not the discovery of ontological reality (we discuss ontology in greater detail in the next section). A *constructivist* philosophy would reject absolutism in epistemology. Glasersfeld believes that both the above principles need to be adopted for the theory to be effective. He maintains that constructivism breaks with convention and develops a theory of knowledge in which knowledge does not reflect an 'objective' ontological reality, but exclusively builds an ordering and organization of a world constituted by our experience. In the construction of knowledge, communication, negotiation and the sharing of meaning play an important part. In the context of action research, Ernest's (1991) case for 'social constructivism' is a perspective which is worthy of consideration (social constructivism is discussed further in Chapter 6). He explains its features:

> First of all, there is the active construction of knowledge, typically concepts and hypotheses, on the basis of experiences and previous knowledge. These provide the basis for understanding and serve the purpose of guiding future actions. Secondly, there is the essential role played by experience and interaction with the physical and social worlds, in both physical and speech modes.

Action researchers are actively engaged in a process of *construction*. Their constructions are based on all the data they collect. They negotiate meanings which will emerge from their interpretations. This position makes them work within the *constructivist* perspective. They are active *'social constructivists'* (Ernest, 1991) because they develop their understandings from communicating with people in their educational settings. As constructivists, they will not be claiming that what they interpret and present are 'whole, absolute truths', but meanings of what they see and hear. Their constructions will be affected by their ideas and values and by the context they work in. In a very illuminating chapter in the *Handbook of Action Research*, Lincoln (2001: 130) states that there are several profound and sympathetic connections between constructivist inquiry and action research. She believes that:

> much of the epistemological, ontological and axiological belief systems is the same or similar, and methodologically, constructivists and action researchers work in similar ways, relying on qualitative methods in face-to-face work, while buttressing information, data and background with quantitative method work when necessary or useful.

Making your philosophical stance known

When selecting and making a decision about what methodology to use, researchers need to consider their ontological and epistemological stance. Whichever philosophical stance we take it is important to declare this and understand the implications of our chosen stance with regard to data collection and analysis. In order to do that we take closer look, in the next section, at what the different theoretical perspectives mean within the context of action research. Further readings on these topics are provided at the end of this chapter.

Ontological issues

Ontology (theory of being) refers to the claims or assumptions about the nature of *social reality* – about what exists, what it looks like, what units make it up and how these units interact with each other (Blaikie, 1993: 6). Within action research, researchers would consider this reality as socially constructed and not external and independent. Meaningful construction occurs both through interpretations of a researcher's experiences and through communica-tion. The stories they tell will be based on subjective accounts from people who live within their environment. The methods of data collection they use will be consistent with their ontological stance. Action researchers must make their theoretical stance clear at the start and also at the dissemination stage.

At this point I will illustrate the challenge of addressing an ontological perspective in your research with an example. A teacher who was concerned with increasing her pupils' motivation and enthusiasm for learning decided to introduce *learning diaries* which the children could take home. They were invited to record their reactions to the day's lessons and what they had learnt. The teacher reported in her field diary that the learning diaries stimulated the children's interest in her lessons, increased their capacity to learn and generally improved their level of participation in lessons. The challenge for the teacher here is in the analysis and interpretation of the multiplicity of factors accompanying the use of diaries. The diaries were taken home so the entries may have been influenced by discussions with parents. Another possibility is that children felt the need to please their teacher. Another possible influence was that their increased motivation was as a result of the difference in style of teaching which included more discussions in the classroom based on the entries in the dairies.

Unlike positivist researchers, this teacher can only claim the influence of introducing the learning diaries within her context, based on her interpretations and reflections. Her personal judgement will be tentative and awaiting further support from others. Your claims will need to take the other factors into account and you need to acknowledge these in your communications. Another challenge for you as an action researcher working in a social context is that your beliefs and values may conflict with those of others in the cultural settings and practices. I experienced this first-hand while working with a teacher who was trying to introduce an interactive style of teaching to a school in the Far East where, according to my student, they follow the principle that 'teachers teach and children learn' and so an interactive learning style was not encouraged. Although the teacher was involved in an individual enquiry, she had to face the fact that all learning takes place in a social context and in her reporting stage she acknowledged the tensions and conflicts she experienced in the pursuit of her enquiry and the success she attributed to her change of style in teaching.

Epistemological issues

Epistemology is the theory of knowledge and it presents a view and justification for what can be regarded as knowledge – what can be known and what criteria knowledge must satisfy in order to be called knowledge rather than beliefs (Blaikie, 1993: 7). For traditional researchers, knowledge is certain and it can be discovered through scientific means. For an action researcher, the nature of knowledge and what constitutes knowledge are different. The type of data collected is more subjective where experience and insights are of a unique and personal nature (Burrell and Morgan, 1979). What people say and how we interpret what they do and say are important for an action researcher for knowledge creation.

To illustrate the epistemological challenges within action research, I will use another example here. A teacher of 11 year old children decided to carry out an action research project which involved a change in style in teaching mathematics. Instead of giving children mathematical tasks displaying the subject as abstract principles, she made links with other subjects which she believed would encourage children to see mathematics as a discipline that could improve their understanding of the environment and historic events. At the conclusion of the project, the teacher reported that applicable mathematics generated greater enthusiasm and understanding of the subject.

Here the researcher was involved in a personal enquiry which was aimed at improving an aspect of her practice. She had generated new knowledge, which could then be shared with colleagues in her institution and others in the profession. The knowledge that had been generated about the extent to which mathematics learning had improved would be based on her personal interpretations and supported by the observed enthusiasm of her pupils and what her colleagues may have observed and interpreted. In this instance the action researcher is not like a positivist researcher who may have used scientific methods in the form of test results to make claims to generate knowledge which they consider to be certain. For an action researcher working within a social context the knowledge generated is not certain; it is based on the observation of behaviours and responses from participants – students, colleagues, Critical Friends and personal interpretations. Outcomes will need to be continually refined on the basis of experience, discussion and the negotiation of meanings. The results cannot be generalized, but other professionals may be able to replicate the project and generate similar outcomes. Your philosophical stance will have a bearing on the way you analyse and present your data and the knowledge you generate (see Chapter 6).

The advantages of using action research as a methodology

I conclude this chapter by considering the advantages of using action research as a methodology for researching into aspects of practice. I believe action research is a powerful and useful model for practitioner research because:

- research can be set within a specific context or situation;
- researchers can be participants – they don't have to be *distant* and *detached* from the situation;
- it involves continuous evaluation and modifications can be made as the project progresses;
- there are opportunities for theory to emerge from the research rather than always follow a previously formulated theory;
- the study can lead to open-ended outcomes;
- through action research, a researcher can bring a story to life.

Finally, are there any limitations and disadvantages to using this methodology? When you consider action research for the purposes of professional development or improving a situation, it is difficult to list that many disadvantages. However, action research is sometimes described as a *soft option* by some, so you will need to define the parameters of your study at the start. Gaining insights and planning action are two of the main purposes of being engaged in action research. There is also the issue of ethical considerations which are of particular significance within action research. Such issues are discussed in Chapter 5.

☐ Summary

In this chapter I have tried to give the reader an overview of what doing action research entails. The presentation of models of action research can give but a hint of the flavour of the experience; to digest the nature of action research you need to be an active participant. The key academic researchers who have contributed to the development and more widespread acceptance of action research were indicated, their names and publications cited as landmarks in the progress of the methodology. A salient feature of action research is its cyclical structure and this was highlighted by the diagrammatic forms in which renowned researchers have portrayed their approach to action research. Different readers will, indeed, react to each diagram differently and use them as they see fit within their own action plans. The definitions emphasized the role of action research which is possible within the professional and institutional enhancement of the researchers; the attributes and advantages of action research supported the positive approach readers were encouraged to adopt. As for the four case studies of action research, these were provided as examples, enabling readers to become acquainted with the processes and stages prior to experiencing them personally. Some theoretical underpinnings associated with action research were briefly presented. The chapter concluded with a list of the advantages provided when using action research as a methodology.

Further Reading

Baumfield, V., Hall, E. and Wall, K. (2008) *Action Research in the Classroom.* London: SAGE.

Bell, J. (1999) *Doing Your Research Project.* Buckingham: Open University Press.

Carr, W. and Kemmis, S. (1986) *Becoming Critical: Education, Knowledge and Action Research.* Brighton: Falmer.

Cohen, L., Manion, L. and Morrison, K. (2007) *Research Methods in Education* (6th edn). London: RoutledgeFalmer.

Crotty, M. (1998) *The Foundations of Social Research: Meaning and Perspectives in the Research Process.* London: SAGE

Denscombe, M. (1998) *The Good Research Guide for Small-Scale Social Research Projects.* Buckingham: Open University Press.

Elliott, J. (2006) *Reflecting Where the Action Is.* London: Routledge.

Hopkins, D. (2002) *A Teacher's Guide to Classroom Research* (3rd edn). Buckingham: Open University Press.

McNiff, J. and Whitehead, J. (2005) *All You Need To Know About Action Research*. London: SAGE.

Reason, P. and Bradbury, H. (eds) (2007) *Handbook of Action Research: Participative Inquiry and Practice* (3rd edn). London: SAGE.

Taber, K. (2008) *Classroom-based Research and Evidence–based Practice*: *A guide to Teachers*. London: SAGE.

Taylor, S. (ed.) (2000) *Sociology: Issues and Debates*. Hampshire: Palgrave.

Useful websites

- The Standards Site – www.standards.dcsf.gov.uk/research
  - o This UK government website provides summaries of the latest research and case studies.
- The National Foundation for Educational Research – www.nfer.ac.uk
  - o Provides research summaries and reports of recent research projects.
- Action Research – www.actionresearch.net
  - o An academic journal which published studies of interest to action researchers.
- The Collaborative Action Research Network – www.did.stu.mmu.ac.uk/carn
  - o Provides details of research publications and research conferences.
- Educational Action Research – www.tandf.co.uk/journals/titles
  - o Gives details of Educational Action Research Journal.

2

Getting started

This chapter focuses on:

- the role of action research in professional development;
- the contexts for action research;
- the concerns relating to the usefulness of action research;
- planning an action research project, in practical steps.

In Chapter 1, we explored some features of action research and considered why these features make it a powerful mode of enquiry for practitioners. You should, by now, have a good understanding of the principles which underlie action research and its role in enabling practitioners to improve their practice through a process of reflection. The strongest message that I hope you have received so far is that the principal aim of carrying out an action research project is to support a researcher or group of researchers to study an aspect of practice in depth and learn from the experiences. The knowledge generated from such experiences contributes to the professional development and improvement of practice of the researcher; it also adds to the knowledge base on enhancing quality of learning, when these experiences are shared with others. This chapter focuses on the practical aspects of embarking on an action research project. I will try to demonstrate to you, that with proper guidance and careful planning, all practitioners can undertake action research and enjoy the whole experience.

Before you get started on your action research project, and whatever your professional context, it would be useful for you to consider the following questions:

- What are the features of action research which make it a suitable mode of enquiry for practitioners?
- What are the processes involved in carrying out action research?
- What specific contexts lend themselves to selecting action research as a method of enquiry?

A close look at the above questions should enable you to consider whether you can justify opting for action research as your chosen methodology, so as to engage in fruitful discussions about your activities. If you are a student undertaking an action research project as part of an undergraduate or postgraduate course, you would be expected to demonstrate that you have considered the above questions before embarking on your study.

Action research and professional development

At this point, let us take a moment to consider the salient features of action research, which make it a useful methodology for practitioners. We can begin by sharing Carr and Kemmis's (1986) list of what action research entails. In their seminal work *Becoming Critical*, they view action research as an integral part of critical professional development. The authors list five particular features of action research as a methodology for practitioners. Each of these warrants careful thought and consideration before you take your first step. Some of these ideas were touched on in Chapter 1, but are reinforced here with supporting statements.

So, what are these five features? First, the authors assert that action research will entail indicating how it rejects positivist notions of rationality, objectivity and truth in favour of a dialectical view of rationality. Second, it will entail indicating how action research employs the interpretive categories of teachers by using them as a basis for 'language frameworks' which teachers explore and develop in their own theorizing. Third, action research provides a means by which distorted self-understandings may be overcome by teachers analysing the way their own practices and understandings are shaped, and the fourth is the linking of reflection to action, offering teachers and others a way of becoming aware of how those aspects of the social order which frustrate rational change may be overcome. Finally, it involves returning to the question of theory and practice, to show that self-critical communities of action researchers enact a form of social organization in which truth is determined by the way it relates to practice. Carr and Kemmis's (1986: 162) definition of action research reflects these sentiments:

> A form of enquiry undertaken by participants in social situations in order to improve rationality and justice of their own social or educational practices, as well as their own understanding of these practices and situations in which these practices are carried out.

Let us now consider an all important question: why would a practitioner carry out action research? I can think of several reasons. First, teaching is not about developing a set of technical competencies, although teachers who work with me often say that it is going in that direction! Teaching is concerned with developing young people's minds. This can only be done effectively if the teacher takes time to internalize ideas and this internalisation is more likely to be more effective if it is accompanied by reflection. In recent years the importance of being a reflective practitioner as part of one's professional development has been stressed, not only in the teaching profession, but also for other practitioners in other disciplines – for example social workers and medical workers, to name but a few. The idea of the teacher's effectiveness being enhanced by being a researcher and being engaged in critical reflection was strongly argued by Stenhouse (1975: 143). He was of the opinion that:

> all well founded curriculum research and development, whether the work of an individual teacher, of a school, of a group working at a teachers' centre or a group working within the co-ordinating framework of a national project, is based on the study of classrooms.

Hopkins (2002: 66) offers a useful dimension to the purpose of carrying out action research. He maintains that 'when we are engaged in classroom research, we can be said to be engaged in educational theorizing, because we are reflecting systematically and critically on practice'. This view helps to dispel the unease felt by many that educational theory which one reads only is too remote from practice. Hopkins quotes two of the fundamental aspects of what Schön (1991) describes as the 'reflective practitioner'. In educational terms, he points out that such professional teachers (a) stand in control of knowledge rather than being subservient to it and (b) by doing this they are engaged in the process of theorizing and achieving self-knowledge. Others, such as Hargreaves (1996), have emphasized the concept of teaching as a research-based profession and the importance of evidence-based practice. My own experience with both practitioners and students bears testimony to the freshness and enthusiasm shown by those who have carried out action research and have had opportunities to develop their thinking, and to evaluate and reflect on their practice. The two projects described below, involving innovative and radical changes in teaching styles, demonstrate the passion of two action researchers in Asian countries.

Example

Introducing concept maps to enhance children's understanding of mathematical and scientific concepts

I am a teacher from India, who carried out an action research project in my classroom with 32 eight year olds. The reason I undertook this project is because I felt that my teaching style is very traditional. I stand in front of the class and teach them new topics; some of my students understand the ideas and many don't. When I mark their work, I can spot which of them have really understood what I am teaching and which have not. Students held many misconceptions about mathematical and scientific topics, which were reflected in the mistakes they were making.

My action research was to investigate whether drawing conceptual maps about topics could improve their conceptual understanding of topics. This is something I read in a professional journal where a teacher claimed that it worked in her class. I felt it was worth trying this. The action involved asking children to draw a conceptual map of

(Continued)

(Continued)

what they knew about a topic before a lesson. For example, before I taught multiplication to the class, all the children were asked to write down ideas and words that came to mind about the topic and to draw arrows to make connections between the ideas if they could spot any. I told them we would refer to them as 'concept maps'. The children were taken aback (as they told me, when I interviewed them) but they liked the idea of drawing maps and writing words in a mathematics lesson as it was fun. After teaching multiplication for four sessions, I asked them to write down those words and ideas which they had learned but did not know before the teaching sessions and to do these in a different colour. To add to their surprise, I deviated from the usual style of teaching and asked them to share their concept maps with the person sitting next to them. Dates were written on the conceptual maps (before and after the lessons).

I wanted to keep the data collection simple. I collected and analysed the conceptual maps. I also analysed children's written work and the number of mistakes they made. I interviewed a small number of children about the mistakes they made to gain insights into what the level of misunderstandings were, so that I could address these in my teaching.

The results were pleasing. Children made fewer mistakes. The concept maps showed that children had made interconnections between concepts; for example, they had drawn arrows between addition and multiplication showing an understanding of multiplication as repeated addition.

What did I learn? I now know the concept maps are a good idea. The innovative visual representations involved in the concept maps introduced a physical aspect into what are abstract processes. I think I am convinced that you can change your teaching style without losing class control, as my children behaved impeccably and learnt more. At the outset, I realized that I had to abandon the idea of introducing concept maps in two subjects at the same time, as it was unmanageable for data collection and analysis. The purpose of the research was to enhance students' conceptual understanding and this was achieved. It was quite an anxious time for me to employ a different teaching style in our school setting, but the results made it all worthwhile. I feel I am a better teacher now. My colleagues and I now intend to try this idea in teaching science.

Example

Transmission or interaction? An action research project undertaken in China

I am a teacher from China. This is a short summary of my action research which I carried out in my classroom as part of my Master's programme. I am used to a transmission model of teaching where I teach and children listen. I have no discipline problems. I prepare my lessons and go through all the points. Students take notes

(Continued)

(Continued)

carefully. At the end of the lesson I ask questions to verify that the students have learnt what I have taught and most of the questions I ask are answered correctly.

My research question was formulated after a considerable amount of discussion with my university tutor. The question was: Can an interactive style of teaching enhance the learning of my students? I selected this topic because of a film I watched during a lecture which showed discussion and interaction in lessons, at different levels. The teacher in the film was engaged in interactive discussions during his teaching. Students were working in small groups and discussing ideas. There seemed to be a very lively environment in the classroom and the students were enthusiastic about what they were learning. They were quite animated during discussions. My first concern was whether I would be able to import this style of teaching into a cultural context where students are not used to raising questions and being involved in extensive discussions. Another problem was whether I would be able to get through the syllabus using this style of teaching. Would I be able to keep discipline? I decided to explore the possible benefits and potential problems of this style of teaching.

I planned my teaching lessons carefully, introducing group discussions gradually. Students were encouraged to ask questions during the teaching sessions if they wished to. At the end of a lesson, I gave the students time to prepare short presentations, in groups, which included answering two questions:

- What did you learn in the session?
- What did you think of the way you were taught?

I collected my data mainly by using observations, some of which were by recording the sessions which were then watched by my colleagues and myself. I kept my own personal learning journal, where I made a note of all significant aspects of the changes in my teaching and the changes in the students.

I found out that there was more enthusiasm for learning among my students. There was a buzz in the classroom. There were more smiles on their faces. I was pleased with these outcomes. However, there was some anxiety among some members of the other teaching staff who, like me, were used to a different style of teaching. They, like the parents and grandparents of my students, needed convincing that a new method of teaching was worth exploring. This was a challenge. The parents did comment on the greater motivation and confidence shown by their children, but were not quite sure why I was doing this. I needed to explain my reasons to them in the next stage of my work.

What have I learnt? I have learnt that a transmission model of teaching is suitable for teaching facts and skills. But to instil curiosity and enthusiasm for learning, I need to allow my students greater freedom of enquiry and discussions with me and among themselves, if I wish to encourage creative thinking. Social interaction between the students was found to create collective understanding leading to personal acquisition of knowledge. The knowledge I myself have acquired by introducing an

(Continued)

(Continued)

innovative teaching method has provided me with some new insights into the process of teaching and learning. In the next cycle of my project, I need to find out whether my new style has raised students' achievement in tests. My new hunch, or hypothesis, is that the new methodology may encourage my students to write more creatively and also to demonstrate more developed problem-solving strategies. I will explore this hunch in the next stage of my research, perhaps with a few more willing teachers involved, and do this as part of my doctoral work.

What are the processes and outcomes of action research?

Before moving on to the practical task of planning an action research project, let us consider the basic tenets of action research as described by O'Leary (2004: 139), who defines action research as:

> A strategy that pursues action and knowledge in an integrated fashion through a cyclical and participatory process. In action research, processes, outcome and application are inextricably linked.

Here is a task for you. Suppose you are considering carrying out an action research project. Indeed you may already have a few ideas in mind. Try to consider to what extent your project would involve the following summarized list of processes within action research, as put forward by O'Leary (2004: 139). For each section, you could pose some questions relating it to your topic and initial plans. Writing your thoughts down would be helpful.

- *Addresses practical problems.* It generally involves the identification of practical problems in a specific context and an attempt to seek and implement solutions within that context. As the project is situated within the workplace, the ownership of change is a priority and the goal is to improve professional practice.
- *Generates knowledge.* The purpose is the production of knowledge to produce change and the enacting of change to produce knowledge.
- *Enacts change.* Changes are incorporated into immediate goals and not left to be implemented after the project.
- *Is participatory.* In action research, researchers collaborate with practitioners and other stakeholders. Contrary to many other research paradigms, action research works *with* rather than *on* or *for* the researched.
- *Is a cyclical process.* Action research is a cyclical process that takes shape as knowledge emerges. Cycles converge towards better situational understanding and improved action implementation, and are based in evaluative practice that alternates between action and critical reflection.

It would also be helpful to remind ourselves of the evolutionary nature of action research, as described by Reason and Bradbury (2001: 2):

> since action research starts with everyday experience and is concerned with the development of living knowledge, in many ways the process of inquiry is as important as specific outcomes. Good action research emerges over time in an evolutionary and developmental process, as individuals develop skills of inquiry and as communities of inquiry develop within communities of practice.

Reason and Bradbury (2001: 449) also stress the importance of continuing dialogue between the members of the action research communities of inquiry:

> In a pluralist community of inquiry – whether it be a face-to-face inquiry group, an organization, or community – different individual members are likely to hold different questions with different degrees of interest. Some will be most concerned with relationships, some with action, some with understanding, some with raising awareness. To the extent that dialogue is encouraged between these different perspectives the quality of the inquiry will be increased. We would argue that it is important for the action research team or community of inquiry as a whole, to take time regularly for reflection on the choice points made along the way and the possible need for re-orientation from time to time.

Having considered the processes involved, we can now move on to look at the contexts for action research.

Contexts for action

A recent review of published case studies on websites (see useful websites at the end of Chapter 1), journals and those carried out by my own students showed that educational action researchers come from a variety of backgrounds and their topics of study draw on a wide range of subjects. The following examples of action research projects demonstrate the range of topics for action research.

Enhancing classroom practice

These are some studies carried out by teachers in their classrooms which focus on an aspect of their practice. Examples are:

- How can I encourage more discussion in my classroom? Who does most of the talking in my class – the children or me?
- How can I improve my questioning skills?

- How can I improve children's participation in Information and Communication Technology?
- Will the introduction of a 'learning diary' in science lessons enhance children's conceptual understanding?
- Can the introduction of personal research projects focusing on children's special interests enhance students' learning?

Research relating to a particular educational theme

With new initiatives being announced with increasing frequency by governments world-wide, action research offers practitioners an opportunity to explore new ideas and evaluate them systematically. Here are some examples:

- What is *personalized learning* and how can I implement it in my classroom?
- Does the teaching of problem-solving skills enhance children's performance in other areas of their work?
- What is meant by creativity in the classroom? What is creativity and how can I encourage children to be creative?
- I attended a conference on 'Multiple Intelligences' as a theory of perceiving ability which can be used as a basis for talent development. How do I put this into practice?
- Can the discrete teaching of critical thinking skills raise achievement in different subject areas?
- How can we enhance the motivation of our students?

Institutional focus

These are some topics based in the workplace, such as:

- How can we increase participation at parents' meetings?
- How can we encourage more discussion during staff meetings?
- Can we devise a new record-keeping system which is more manageable and useful?
- How can we develop a more caring ethos in the school?
- How can we make school-based, in-service sessions more effective?
- Are our citizenship lessons having any impact on students' behaviour?
- Devise anti-bullying strategies, monitor their effectiveness and design a school policy.

Implementation of a new initiative arising from new policy or research

Action research is often carried out by a group of practitioners who will select a new initiative, study its practical implications and make decisions based on the collective experiences of the participants. Examples are:

- Setting up a 'learning mentor scheme' responding to a government recommendation, investigating its practical implications and producing a set of guidelines for schools on how to implement the scheme effectively.
- Adopting the new *assessment for learning* framework.
- An exploration, by university tutors, of how to increase the number of students from poorer backgrounds enrolling at university.

Action research as purposeful research

I quoted the views of one practising teacher, Laura, in the Introduction to this book, who used to feel that research was for the lucky few who pursued academic careers. Carrying out an action research project brought it home to her that it was possible for practising teachers to experience the research process and benefit from that experience. In recent years, concern has been expressed by some (Hargreaves, 1996; Rose, 2002) that education research was not always reaching practitioners, as quite often work produced by academics was published in journals which are generally not read by practitioners. In this context, it is worth pointing out that action research opens up opportunities for practitioners to actually be involved in research which has an immediate relevance and application. There has been an increase in the number of action research projects carried out by practitioners around the world; this is reflected in the increasing number of presentations based on action research in the American and the British Educational Research Association conference presentations (AERA and BERA – see websites). A study of the stated aims of the teacher-researcher scheme (1997–2001) offered by the Teacher Training Agency (1998) in the United Kingdom is one example of the many efforts being made by governments to make teaching a research-based profession. The aims of the teacher-researcher scheme presented below are worthy of consideration, for practitioners starting out on their action research.

- To encourage teachers to engage with research and evidence about pupils' achievements, for example to use other people's research to inform their practice and/or to participate actively in research.
- To increase the capacity for high-quality, teacher-focused classroom research by supporting teacher involvement in the development of research proposals for external funding.
- To support teachers in designing, applying and carrying out more medium and large-scale classroom-based research about pedagogy where teachers have an active role.
- To enable experiments in disseminating research findings and making use of them in classrooms.
- To provide examples of good practice in making use of research.

Is action research real research?

Before starting out, the action researcher should also be aware of some of the criticisms raised against action research and how these can be dealt with in the context of both setting up a project and disseminating the outcomes. What are the concerns raised by critics? Let us consider each of the following headings and respond to these concerns.

• *Concern 1: Action research lacks rigour and validity*

Questions are sometimes raised on issues regarding the validity of findings. You may be asked: how can you achieve objectivity when you are researching your own practice? There are ways of dealing with this. First, you would need to acknowledge your values and epistemological stance right from the start. You would be setting up a validation group to share your data with (see Chapter 6) before generating evidence from your findings. You need to be rigorous in both gathering and analysing data within action research. In all action research, the fieldwork is located within one's own context and should be acknowledged as such. Remember, you are not drawing on national samples of data here. Sharing data with critical friends and using triangulation would also ensure that the quality of what is gathered is robust and without bias.

• *Concern 2: Action research findings are not generalisable*

Many of my students have been anxious about the issue of generalisability within action research. My argument is that the action researcher does not set out to seek generalisable data, but to generate knowledge based on action within one's own situation. The researcher would be asking 'What am I doing here?' and 'How can I improve my practice?'. Any findings from the research are generalisable only within that situation and within the context of the work and the researcher's beliefs, which are declared in advance. Dissemination of findings could be applicable to those who are interested and to other practitioners in similar circumstances, either locally or at a distance. It may also be useful for those who wish to apply the ideas and findings within similar contexts or replicate the study. I always compare the dissemination of a case study within an action research project to showing a documentary for raising issues; this can be very powerful.

• *Concern 3: It is a deficit model*

Quite often, reference is made to the problem-solving nature of action research which may portray the process as a deficit model. As previously stated, the research questions and topics arise from your desire to improve practice. The topic of exploration may not be giving you any problem at all. If you are trying to solve a problem, however, developing strategies for solving a problem within a situation is surely not a negative reaction! It really is about making progress and developing innovative ideas and strategies.

Making a start

Whether you are a practitioner intending to carry out research within your institution or an undergraduate or postgraduate student planning a topic for a special study which leads to a dissertation, thorough planning can reduce much of the anxiety you may feel at the start. Although most of the models of action research presented in Chapter 1 describe action research as being cyclical in nature, my students often tell me that some awareness of what may happen during the project, represented in distinct stages, helps them to have an overview of the whole process and to plan more efficiently. But you need to bear in mind that any model of suggested progression does not always necessarily guarantee that your project will follow that order. It is simply helpful to think about the stages in order to gain some insight into what to expect. So, what might these stages be? The following list may be helpful.

- Identifying a topic and setting the context.
- Reviewing and analysing the literature.
- Focusing on a topic, formulating a research question or hypothesis.
- Planning activities.
- Implementing, acting.
- Gathering and analysing data.
- Analysing the data further.
- Reflecting on outcomes and generating evidence.
- Reporting findings.

Rather than dealing with the above stages separately, I will try to discuss these stages under three broad headings.

i.   Identifying a topic.
ii. Moving on.
iii. Practical considerations.

Identifying a topic

The first task for an action researcher or a group of researchers is to select a topic for investigation or enquiry. It is very likely that you have not yet come to a decision on what to study. It is perfectly natural for beginner researchers to have a number of topics in mind. It is often useful to write these down. Your ideas may have come to you from a number of contexts. It may be that you have read an article or a book about a new aspect or approach. Often, a new directive from the government can spark researchers' interest in looking at its implications in practice. It is possible that your interest in exploring a topic arose as a result of being given a new responsibility for a particular subject area or because you had been placed within a new managerial role. Or, as a teacher-trainee, you may have several ideas buzzing around in your head that you want to explore. In some cases you may be asked by the authorities within an education district or your own institution to undertake research in order to evaluate the effectiveness of a particular initiative or a new theme and suggest modifications. In all these cases, one thing that is common is the relevance of your research to your professional development.

Taking the first step

If you are in the process of selecting a topic for research, it is a good idea to write out a list of all the topics which are of interest to you before selecting one that you feel strongly about – this will often be something which is very personal to you. During the introductory session on action research, I usually ask my students to write down their first thoughts on various topics and to explain why they feel these topics are important to them. Students first talk about their initial choices in groups, and they do find this a useful process in helping them to focus on a particular topic or aspect of a topic. Here is an example of what Helen, one of my undergraduate students, wrote:

I have *three* topics in mind that I would like to choose from.

1. First is the way my class is grouped into ability groups at present. I wondered if children's attitudes may be affected by being put in a particular group for all the lessons, especially if they are in a lower ability group. Although they are never referred to as lower ability, they often tell me that they are the 'dunce' group and mess about too much. I can see why it is necessary to group them for some lessons, but I want to find out whether their attitude to work and the quality of their work will be different if they work with children who are more able, at least for other lessons. Perhaps I could try a different grouping strategy for topic work ...
2. My second topic is to try some problem-solving activities with children. I feel that the children learn much of what I teach them by rote, and do very little thinking ...
3. The third topic I am interested in is creative writing. A number of children seem to be really turned off during this lesson. I would like to introduce some new stimulus and record any changes in their attitude and in what they produce ...

Rachel, a secondary school teacher who was planning to apply for external funding from the government for an action research project, wrote:

As I am the co-ordinator for Information Technology, I want to work on something to do with IT, but I am not sure what, yet. Here are some thoughts.

- The first question: Do students make good use of the IT facilities in the school?
- Second one: How I can improve students' use of the Internet for their project work? At the moment they seem to just print out so much, but do not actually know how to make use of all the information.
- The third one is about assessing the effectiveness of ICT software packages that we buy. There are so many companies producing software and different departments in our school buy them, but we have never really evaluated their usefulness or how we can make effective use of these packages. I would like to set up a research framework to explore the effectiveness of these potentially useful resources.

After talking through her ideas with other members of the group who also raised questions, Helen decided to undertake a study of the creative writing topic. The discussion of Rachel's ideas took a long time. It was interesting to see Rachel being challenged on the very general nature of her first idea as not being feasible within a relatively short period of time. Rachel's third idea involving several departments, again, was felt to be difficult to carry out within the time constraints of a funded project lasting just a few months. So, she decided to focus on evaluating software in just one subject systemically by collecting and analysing appropriate data.

Discussing your ideas with others can often help focus your thoughts on considering the feasibility of carrying out a study on a particular topic, its sensitivity and the practical implications. Finally, it may be the case that you decide to select your action research topic for other reasons. For example, you may be facing dilemmas about something – perhaps whether to use a particular published scheme or resource or to improve the recording of assessment within your classroom.

Critical appraisal of topics for action research

As part of a research training session, one of my colleagues and I asked our students to comment on the possibility of undertaking action research on the following topics. Some of these were chosen deliberately to generate discussions – and in some cases these proved very heated! Study each of these (you may want to do this with one or two colleagues) and try to write down some of your comments before reading the examples that we gathered from our students during the session. This exercise was not designed to provide definitive answers, but to promote the exchange of ideas.

i.   Factors contributing to effective learning.
ii. Implementing an accelerated learning model in my classroom.
iii. Improving my questioning strategies.

iv.   Monitoring the bullying of women teachers in my institution by male teachers.
v.   A comparison of mathematics performance test results across three local education authorities in our neighbourhood.
vi.   Extending able children through after-school activities.

Commentary

i.   The first topic was considered too general for an action research project in its existing form. It was suggested that the researcher could identify factors that contributed to effective learning from existing research or other literature and plan one or two intervention activities based on these factors. The activities could be presented to a selected group of pupils and their progress would then be monitored. The importance of keeping the project small and focused was stressed. So was the challenge of designing a method for judging the effectiveness of strategies for effective learning.
ii.   Accelerated learning strategies have been the subject of many conferences in recent years and it was felt that action research offered an ideal way for implementing the principles and continuously monitoring what was happening. Action research provided opportunities for the researcher to refine strategies and make adjustments as the project progressed. It was felt that this topic would provide opportunities for dissemination to colleagues, using evidence collected during the project.
iii. The third topic – improving one's questioning strategies – received positive comments in terms of its potential as a subject for action research. The personal nature of the investigation, it was felt, would make it an ideal topic for professional development and the improvement of practice. A need to explain what was meant by 'improving' was stressed and strategies for establishing a baseline of current practice were also felt necessary.
iv.   This topic resulted in the noisiest discussion. Questions were raised which included: *Who says there is bullying by male teachers? How could this be studied anyway? Even if it is true, is it too sensitive a topic to make the findings public? Who is going to co-operate with this kind of topic?*
v.   This topic was described as being beyond the scope of an action research project for several reasons: it would take too long and involve an analysis of much quantitative data. One of the main purposes of carrying out action research – improvement of practice – was also unlikely to take a prominent role within this topic.
vi.   The last topic was found suitable for action research. It could focus on a small, manageable group. What was meant by enrichment activities had to be defined and explanations would need to be provided as to how able children might be selected. This project, they felt, could fit into an action research cycle of selecting a topic, reviewing the existing literature, planning activities, evaluating and reflecting. It provided opportunities for refining the activities when responding to the on-going gathering of evidence.

Fine-tuning the research topic

Having selected a topic for investigation, it may be necessary to consider different aspects of the topic to help you fine-tune it before you start your study. But do remember, many action researchers also recognize the need to fine-tune their topic after reading some related literature or after thinking about the practical implications of carrying out their study.

Here is one example of how a teacher-researcher refined her topic of study. Melanie selected her action research topic: (*Introducing portfolios of learning*) involving her class of 13 year old students. During her discussion with colleagues it was pointed out to her that the topic was too wide for action research. It was suggested that Melanie needed to narrow her focus and perhaps concentrate on one aspect of her topic. She then generated some sub-questions within the general topic of the use of portfolios, such as:

- What are portfolios?
- Do portfolios enhance my pupils' motivation for learning?
- Can I involve parents in developing their children's portfolios?

After some consideration she decided that the third question was more likely to suit the format of action research.

Some examples of topics

In this section I have included various examples of action research projects. Some of these are from my own students and others are examples of projects from other sources that I have read about. The purpose of including them is twofold. First, it shows the range of topics that practitioners have selected for their research and, second, it also shows the different types of titles people have used. Some are in the form of a question, or a hypothesis, and others relate to specific aspects of practice.

- How can I improve communications between staff in my role as a senior manager?
- An enquiry into the feasibility of adopting the Italian 'Reggio Emelia' programme in an Early Years classroom in England.
- Design and evaluation of an intervention programme to enhance children's understanding of doing 'subtraction'.
- Using group work to encourage creativity.
- The use of music as a stimulus for creative writing. What are the outcomes?
- Children in my class – aged 5 years old – making big books and leading class discussions.
- Introducing problem solving in mathematics lessons and monitoring any changes in children's attitudes and achievement in mathematics.
- A study of the attitudes of boys and girls to creative writing and responding to what I find out by planning action.
- Does homework enhance student achievement?
- Developing and evaluating activities which promote talk among children with English as an Additional Language.
- Developing a system for formative feedback in English lessons.
- Can encouraging imagery support mental mathematics?
- What do students feel about their algebra lessons?

Moving on

After selecting a topic, the next set of useful questions to ask are:

- What is currently happening in the area which I intend to investigate?
- What am I expecting from the project?
- What can I actually do about it?
- How would I go about it?
- What information will I need?
- Have I got the resources I require?

One very useful question to consider here is whether or not it will be possible to make any changes that you may wish to *after* the project has been completed. For example, one of my Master's students was feeling uneasy about the introduction of the National Literacy Strategy by the UK government; he was considering undertaking a study, hoping to make recommendations as to whether they should continue to follow the strategy in his school. He realized very quickly that little could be done if he wished to persuade his school to abandon the National Literacy Strategy, and that his time and efforts would be better employed working on ways to make the strategy more effective in terms of children's motivation and learning.

Similarly, if it is your local education board's policy to set targets for all its schools, any effort spent on an action research project to resist this may be a waste of energy and valuable time. However, I am not discouraging you here from undertaking research in controversial areas, as long as the purpose is a greater understanding of issues relating to a topic or the identification of factors which could lead to fruitful discussions with others who may be interested. In relation to the National Literacy Strategy, for example, any contribution in terms of an analysis of its purpose and the practical aspects of its delivery could be of immense value to both policy makers and practitioners.

Practical considerations

In this section we will look at some other practical issues that an action researcher needs to consider.

Experience and interest

A topic for action research will often be located within a researcher's experience and context and it needs to be grounded in the realities of the workplace. Ask yourself if you are sufficiently interested in the topic of investigation to devote a considerable amount of time and effort to it. In my experience, I find a personal interest and passion for a topic to be important factors which motivate action researchers. I have witnessed many animated action researchers who have carried out enquiries on subjects which were meaningful and relevant to their situations.

The research question

If your action research involves investigating a question, you need to consider the type of question which is appropriate to ask. A consideration of what your expected outcomes are may help you in phrasing this question. You will need to consider whether your question is specific or open-ended in nature. You may wish to explore a specific question and expect multiple outcomes from your project. It may be that you have a hypothesis to explore. A hypothesis can be based on a tentative, speculative conjecture about an issue which you wish to investigate, or it may be based on an intuitive insight about an idea which then needs to be explored. I always feel that a hypothesis arising from the curiosity of the researcher is worthy of investigation, but I would also emphasize the importance of data-gathering within the context of action research. You need to be open-minded in your collection and analysis of data, but to also bear in mind what kind of data need to be collected in order to draw any conclusions.

Scope and resources

Remember that an action research project needs to be focused and that quite often these are small-scale investigations. You will need to select topics which are manageable and which support your professional development. I often tell my students that they are not likely to change the world through an action research project, but may bring about an improvement in their own practice or implement some changes within their institution and support those who read or hear about the project to replicate it. Ask yourself what you can possibly achieve in the timescale available to you. Be realistic. You also need to consider any external factors that may affect the project. For example, do you have enough resources to carry out your project? Consider this question in terms of the availability of time, people and physical materials. Do you, for example, have support for word processing or transcribing tapes? You also need to consider whether you are likely to change your job during the scheduled time of the project or if your institution intends to embark on another initiative which will require your time.

Planning

The importance of planning cannot be overemphasized. Make your aims clear and list your objectives unambiguously. Plan activities which relate to the achievement of your objectives. Spend time considering the kind of data you will need to collect and the processes involved in the data collection. It is also important to think about how you may analyse and validate your data (see Chapter 6). It is useful to initiate a literature search as soon as you have a selected a topic for consideration and to start making notes and summaries. In the light of what you read, it may be necessary for you to refine or even change your topic.

Working collaboratively

An important feature of action research is that it can offer opportunities for collaborative work. The need for collaboration and co-operation is of paramount importance for the success of your project. You may be part of a group of action researchers, in which case whether you are leading the project or contributing to it teamwork is essential. If you are in a leadership role, it is important to show that you value everyone's contributions. If you are a co-researcher it will be necessary to listen and share perspectives as often as you can possibly manage this. I encourage my students to set up a list of Critical Friends who are willing to discuss their work, look at the documentation, provide their perspectives and offer advice where possible. The role of Critical Friends is helpful in maintaining the rigour and quality of your findings. But remember that it is not always easy to accept critical comments on what you have spent hours preparing or doing. Establishing trust and respect for your Critical Friends is, therefore, paramount.

Consider dissemination

Finally, do consider the question of what you will do with your findings when the project is complete. It is important, from the start, to think about how you can disseminate the project findings. It may be that you will need to send a report to a funding body. Or there may be a specific format you will need to follow. Are you intending to make a conference presentation or lead a professional development course? Would you consider writing for a professional journal? You may be doing this project as part of your studies at university that will lead to a dissertation. In all these cases, it will be useful to look to the future and think about possible final outcomes. I remember one of my action researchers sharing her folder of children's work and photographs with me. She had been collecting these from the start of the project to use on a course she was subsequently 'expected' to deliver at the local teachers' centre – six months after the project was to be completed.

☐ Summary

In the first half of this chapter I made a case for action research by highlighting its value for educational enhancement. I tried to address some of the criticisms levelled against action research and explained its purpose in terms of improving practice. The five features of action research proposed by Carr and Kemmis may appear complex, but they do provide the essence of what is involved in the search for truth, through action research, and will steer you towards practical benefits for practitioners and

(Continued)

(Continued)

the recipients of the process of education. Also O'Leary's indicators of structure and processes may be linked to the cyclical model depicted in Chapter 1.

The second half of the chapter guided the reader towards the first steps of enquiry into educational reality. The advice provided on the selection of a research topic and its refinement and revision resulting from discussions with colleagues should make a significant contribution to a harmonious, collaborative working environment, whether the action research is to be directed towards an improvement in the performance of an individual, or a practical aspect of implementing new educational initiatives within a classroom, institution or education authority.

Further Reading

McIntyre, D. (2005) 'Bridging the gap between research and practice', *Cambridge Journal of Education*, 35 (3): 357–82.

Denscombe, M. (1998) *The Good Research Guide for Small-scale Social Research Projects*. Buckingham: Open University Press.

Baumfield, V., Hall, E. and Wall, K. (2008) *Action Research in the Classroom*. London: SAGE.

McNiff, J. and Whitehead, J. (2005) *All You Need To Know About Action Research*. London: SAGE.

Useful websites

- American Educational Research Association – http://www.aera.net
- British Educational Research Association – http://www.bera.ac.uk

3
Reviewing the literature

This chapter focuses on:

- the purpose of reviewing relevant literature;
- the kinds of literature to collect;
- searching for literature;
- the sources of literature;
- evaluating sources from the Internet;
- managing your literature;
- reviewing and writing up the literature.

Assume you have selected an area of study for your action research. Your aim is to generate new knowledge and to share your findings with others. It is important for all researchers to get to know what is available relating to the topic they are about to research. You need to find out what is accessible as books, journal papers, policy documents and other sources. You also need to analyse what you find and review this. Although I have included the process of reviewing literature in a defined sequence in Chapter 2 for practical purposes, it is worth remembering here that this review of related literature will support all stages of your action research. A good researcher will start reading about a topic as soon as an idea is being considered for enquiry. Literature reviews should help you to focus on a topic or research question, select appropriate methodology, and structure the discussions and the final writing-up. After you have completed the project, you will still find the literature review useful as you disseminate your findings, whether this is in the form of a written or website report, a dissertation, conference papers or journal articles. As O'Leary (2004: 66) points out, the 'production of new knowledge is fundamentally dependant on past knowledge' and 'it is virtually impossible for researchers to add to a body of literature if they are not conversant with it'. Indeed O'Leary's assertion provides an appropriate background to this chapter:

> ... working with literature is an essential part of the research process. It inspires, informs, educates and enlightens. It generates ideas, helps form significant questions, and is instrumental in the process of research design. It is also central to the process of writing-up; a clear rationale

supported by literature is essential, while a well constructed literature review is an important criterion in establishing researcher credibility.

The purposes of reviewing relevant literature

Why do you need to find out what others have done and discovered in your area of research? Because doing so can help you in several ways. It can enhance your understanding of the issues associated with the topic. It can also help you to sharpen the focus of your study. My students often refine or fine-tune their research question or hypothesis after reading around a topic.

Such efforts will help you to gain insights into the topic as well as guide you in the pursuit of fruitful activities. Time spent searching for relevant literature could in fact optimise the benefits of your research and support you with the structure and quality of your enquiry. Indeed it may help you to decide whether a line of enquiry is appropriate and feasible. Note that I am not discouraging you from pursuing a topic of study which has been researched before, on the assumption that 'there is no need to reinvent the wheel'. If you do find a study similar to the one you are about to undertake, you may decide to replicate it within your own context, using an appropriate set of methods. This might help you to assess whether a set of findings generated from a different study would be applicable to your context. Whatever the outcome of your research, we need to remind ourselves that the action researcher generates knowledge within a professional context as part of continuing professional development.

Here are some more reasons why your literature search and review could help you in your action research. Getting to know the literature relating to your area of study should:

- help you to identify what has been done before and any gaps;
- help you to develop a conceptual understanding of the topic of enquiry;
- provide you with the academic vocabulary used within the topic;
- provide a background to your enquiry and help you to articulate a rationale for the study;
- support you in reviewing and refining your research topic, question or hypothesis;
- enable you to locate your project within current debates and viewpoints;
- provide a backcloth for your study;
- help you to analyse your findings and discuss them with rigour and scholarship.

While it is good to read as much as you can at this point, you still need to be realistic in terms of what you can manage. It is also helpful to consider what exactly is expected of you. Again, your personal circumstances will have some bearing on the decision as to the extent of your literature search.

If you are carrying out action research as part of an accredited study (such as a Master's or a taught doctorate programme) you will be expected to present a comprehensive review of the literature and demonstrate your understanding of the issues around a topic. The research literature should help you to build up a framework for the fieldwork you are about to undertake, as well as provide a basis for a further discussion of the issues after the data have been collected and analysed. You need to be asking how your data will relate to the findings and theories put forward by others. If you are undertaking a small-scale action research project as part of a local initiative or as an externally-funded project, you will still need to read about your topic as it will help you to contextualize your study within the existing literature. In this case you may want to focus on smaller, key readings. So, to summarize, an action researcher needs to undertake a literature search and analysis in order to understand, locate, plan and evaluate a study more effectively.

This chapter will explore the ways in which an action researcher can go about searching for literature – both theory and research – by providing some practical suggestions.

What kinds of literature?

There are various forms of literature you will need to consider. The following sections discuss a selection.

Policy-related literature

This includes official documents which outline the education policy a practitioner needs to be familiar with. For example, a recent major initiative within secondary schools in your country will have several strands to it and you may be researching into one of these strands. If your research topic is to do with, say, the mentoring of students, reading the relevant official documents will help you to understand both the rationale and the context of the initiative. The rationale provided in these official documents – often justified in terms of theory and research – may spark off some new ideas in your mind. You may also discover papers which address the issues around the new initiatives in current professional journals. Recent newspaper articles can also often provide you with insights into new initiatives. These insights could prove useful to you when setting up the context or background for your work.

Theoretical literature

Locating your research within a theoretical background is important too. Even if you are only engaged in a small-scale project, it is extremely useful to locate any of the theoretical views that underlie what you are about to research. If your research forms part of a degree or accredited module, your tutors should provide you with guidance during lectures and give you appropriate reading lists. For example, if your study focuses on the role of adult mentors in enhancing children's learning, you would certainly be advised to read Vygotsky's (1978) work on the Zone of Proximal Development, which explains how a child's potential is more effectively realized with adult support. The theoretical literature can date back several decades, but may still be relevant to your understanding of the topic of enquiry.

Existing research

A third type of literature you could be seeking comprises existing research findings on your chosen topic. Who else may have studied a similar theme? There is a vast amount of research literature available in research journals which are often accessible electronically. These range from large-scale studies to the findings of action research projects carried out by other researchers such as yourself. You will find it useful to read about the research findings of others and also to take note of the methodology they used for their studies. You may wish to focus on the most recent of these sources. The websites of subject associations and professional organizations, as well as government research sites, can be useful sources.

Research methods

When you are reading research literature, take note of the research methods used by other researchers, especially if a study was carried out as action research. You will find these in all academic journals; journals reporting action research projects will be particularly helpful. These will support you with a choice of methods for data gathering and analysis. Make a critical appraisal of the methodology used by others. Ask yourself whether the data-gathering methods were appropriate. Were the data analysed effectively? Were the findings presented clearly and coherently?

Searching for relevant literature

Before considering the various ways in which you can search for literature relating to your study, let me share with you what my students often tell me. One student confided to me that her search for literature generated such a large amount of information that she was quite overwhelmed by it. This is partly the result of the Internet age we live in and the facilities for fast information retrieval. What you need to do is to skim through a document to find out what is being offered and then select a few sources which are directly relevant to your topic of research. (Using Internet-based sources is discussed in more detail later in this chapter.)

So, where do you begin your search of the literature? If you are a student at university undertaking a course for a qualification, or if your small-scale research is supervised by a university tutor, your library would be the most useful and accessible place for you to start. Most libraries have good systems for accessing literature in the form of books and journals; you can also access research papers electronically using key word searches. For example, if your research topic is

'Adult mentoring for the enhancement of learning', using key words such as *mentor* and *adult support* will generate abstracts of papers from national and international journals. You can then decide which papers are directly relevant and useful to your study.

Don't forget that the journals and newsletters of professional organizations are alternative sources for your search. If you are not working within a university, your local library can help you with a literature search through utilising inter-library loans. University-based research and development centres and their websites are also helpful sources of recent information. These publicize conferences and seminars which you may wish to attend in order to listen to experts in the field that you are researching. Education journals and newspapers can also provide information on relevant conferences and courses that you may wish to attend.

As you are about to embark on a search for literature relating to your topic, you may find the following step-by-step suggestions helpful:

- In your initial search – especially if you are undertaking this on the web – you are likely to find a large number of books, chapters in books, journal papers and newspaper articles. Aim to select some key readings within your topic. If you are studying for an accredited course, consult your supervisor and your colleagues first and take their advice. If your work relates to a new policy initiative, then it is imperative that you look at government websites and listings of current conference presentations. Trying to get a balance of books and papers is always a good idea. Publishers are likely to publish key texts in the topic of your research. Try and select refereed papers published in peer-reviewed journals, as these go through rigorous quality procedures.

- Faced with a large number of references to select from, how do you narrow these down to a manageable amount? A practical suggestion here is to select related literature published within seven to ten years ago and read that. You will find that some key sources relating to the historical context of the topic and other significant research findings from the past will be referenced within these papers. You can then track these down as necessary and review them. It is also important for you to have a comprehensive review of the theory and research on your enquiry subject as you are seeking to gain 'expertise' status in the field.

- One very frequently asked question from my students – how many references do I need? – is difficult to answer. It depends on the nature of your enquiry, the nature of the award bearing course you are studying for and how much published literature is available on the subject. The only point I would stress here is that whatever the time scale of your research, you must show that you are aware of any important developments in your topic. As a very rough guide, the number of references used in action research projects that I have supervised have been in the range of 6–15 for small-scale projects, 20 or more for Master's programmes, and 70 or more for professional doctorates which relate specifically to the topic of study (not including references to methodology).

Sources of relevant literature

There are *two* main literature sources you could search for: ***primary sources*** include government publications, policy documents, research papers, dissertations, conference presentations and institutional occasional papers with accounts of research, ***secondary sources*** use primary sources as references, such as papers written for professional conferences and journals, books written for practising professionals and book reviews. Reading secondary sources can often give you a good feel for your topic. You will find both types of literature by searching through the websites of specialist and professional organizations, as well as the websites of academic journals and research conferences such as that of the American Education Research Association (AERA) and British Education Research Association (BERA – see useful websites at the end of this chapter).

Using the Internet

In our Internet age, it is not surprising that this is one of the most useful sources of information. There are several search engines – Google, MSN, Yahoo, to name just a few – and you can use these to search out topic sources by using key words. The downside is that a website will generate thousands of sources which can be overwhelming and you will need to narrow these down via other areas of expertise. Professional organizations will also have websites which can provide you with key sources of books and papers. Remember, you need to evaluate the information you retrieve from these sites and some guidelines are provided below.

Evaluating sources from the Internet

As the Internet provides us with a large range of sources of information, we also need to be aware of ways of evaluating them. Giving a comprehensive list of evaluating criteria is beyond the scope of this book, so I would recommend you go to O' Dochartaigh's (2007) chapter on evaluating Internet sources and how to assess their credibility and authority. For the benefit of a beginning researcher, I am including a set of guidance notes here (based on O' Dochartaigh's book) which may prove useful:

- Find out if the material belongs to an advocacy group. If so, the purpose is to advocate a specific viewpoint or a cause. Whilst many such groups produce work of very high quality and integrity, in some cases and in pursuit of the advancement of a particular point of view such sources may exaggerate claims and distort views. You need to be exceedingly careful when you cite these in your research. Search for alternate views which should also be on the web.
- Academic papers which are published in refereed journals are subject to peer-review and these will probably be recommended by your supervisor. Papers

published on university websites are also subject to quality procedures. But do remember that there are also many papers which you can access on websites which have been included by the authors themselves and which describe their own viewpoints. As these have not always been subject to any reviewing procedures, you will need to be careful and take a critical look at them before choosing to quote from them.

- Although it is important for you to be aware of the current contexts and agendas of educational topics, you also need to employ some caution when you are reviewing newspaper and magazine articles accessed from the web. Remember that news items often take a certain political point of view. The emphasis in the content – of articles and stories – is likely to depend on the editorial position taken, and as a reviewer you need to be aware of this. Consider the objectivity of what is published in these outlets before you accept the literature.

I recommend the reader to consider the following questions, taken once again from the criteria for an evaluation of Internet sources provided by O' Dochartaigh:

- Is it clear who is responsible for the document?
- Is there any information about the person or organization responsible for the page?
- Is there a copyright statement?
- Does it have a print counterpart that reinforces its authority?
- Are the sources clearly listed so they can be verified?
- Is there an editorial input?
- Are the spelling and grammar correct?
- Are biases and affiliations clearly stated?
- Are there dates for when the document was last updated or revised?

Using electronic databases

There are several electronic databases that a researcher can use to search for relevant literature. As there are so many to select from, I will focus here on the most popular ones among educational researchers. The British Education Index will provide you with references for over 400 journals and therefore this should be a very useful starting point for educational researchers. The ERIC (Educational Resources Information Centre) database is one of the largest and most commonly used database for education literature searches. You can do this by using several criteria with keywords – 'Author', 'Title', and so on. If you are searching for papers relating to your research topic – 'peer assessment' – you may search under the terms 'pupil assessment' or 'classroom assessment' first. Using the words 'if' and 'or', you can access sources with both these words (and of course you would also search for 'peer assessment'). By entering these keywords you are likely to generate a larger number of literature sources, but by using the option 'Narrow

My results' you can change the descriptors and options and reduce the number of sources. When you have generated these sources, the next step is to read the abstracts – short summaries of the content of the source – which will provide you with an overview of the findings. If an abstract looks useful, then only you would access the full version of the paper. Using ERIC is not difficult but it does need getting used to and practice, so it may be useful at first to work with someone who has used it before. A library will the best place to visit for support. You may also wish to look at education journal websites for references and abstracts, which are also included in the electronic databases.

Another source which my students find very useful is the EPPI-centre (Evidence for Policy and Practice at the Institute of Education in the UK) where you can access published meta-analysis literature reviews (see the list of websites at the end of this chapter).

Managing your literature review

Organizing your literature

You do need to be systematic in all aspects of managing your literature review. Suppose you have gathered a good range of literature on your topic. Your challenge then is to organize your collection and make it manageable and useful. Bear in mind that you will also need to access your readings at the time of writing-up. Try to be meticulous about keeping a record of what you are reading in terms of references to texts or articles. Organize your summaries of what you have read. I remember various times, during my own doctoral studies, when I wished fervently that I had been more organized with my collection of literature. I used to read and think about the content of what I had read and store a copy of it in a box file, thinking that I would be able to go back later and find the relevant references at the writing-up stage. This strategy proved inefficient and resulted in me wasting a lot of time. As I read more, the more difficult and chaotic it became. As a result it was sometimes very frustrating and time-consuming trying to track down the references I required!

It may sound like stating the obvious, but organizing your literature search efficiently from the start is vital. Here is a practical suggestion using the example of the research topic I used earlier – investigating effective ways in which school mentors can be involved in enhancing children's learning. Suppose you managed to get two journal articles from the library and a print-out of the outline of a similar project from a website. Assume you also obtained a printout an initiative summary from a government website which referred to the role of mentors. After you read its contents you decided to send for the whole document. A further search on the web generated more references on this particular topic. For example, a recent report from the school inspectorate, evaluating the initiative, could be worth sending for. Now you have several references to manage and store.

Storing your literature review

It is important to set up a system which enables you to retrieve all references, right from the beginning. If you are engaged in a small-scale project one of the simplest and most traditional ways of organizing all these sources of information is for you to use index cards. You need to record the title of the book, chapter or paper, the author, date, nature of the content and a short commentary, including any direct quotes you may wish to include later on. The simple examples in Figures 3.1, 3.2 and 3.3 illustrate what I mean.

Author/source: Department for Education and Employment (DfEE)

Title: *Excellence in Cities*

Date: 1999

Description/key issues: Launched by the Labour govt to improve achievement of students in inner-city areas. *Use of 'mentors'* is a key area within this initiative.

Quote: Page ... line ... is useful as a direct quote.

Follow up: Has there been any evaluation of this initiative?

Figure 3.1   Example of recording a reference: a government document

---

Author: Koshy, V.

Title: *Effective Teaching of Numeracy*

Date: 1999

Publisher: Hodder and Stoughton

Description/key issues: This book outlines and critiques the National Numeracy Strategy. Pages 53–78 address issues on mental mathematics. The author deals with some strategies teachers can use for teaching mental mathematics.

Quote: Page 53 – a definition of mental mathematics.

Follow up: The author refers to Askew's Nuffield research project.

Figure 3.2   Example of recording a reference book

Author: Reynolds and Muijs (eds)

Title: *Effective Teaching*

Chapter: 2. Interactive teaching

Publisher: Paul Chapman

Description/key issues: ...

Useful quotes: Page (...)

Follow up: ...

Figure 3.3   Example of recording a chapter in a book

I personally find the use of index cards a very practical and simple way of keeping track of what I have read, but if you have a good knowledge of technology you may be able to set up systems on your computer which will do the same as index cards. In that case, information retrieval and storage will be much quicker. Having said all this, the most effective recording system will be one which is personal and manageable for you. You may want to take note of the above guidelines and then design your own systems. Sorting out your sources of literature into different categories and themes is also helpful.

In recent times you will have had access to software which enables you to store references efficiently. For example, EndNote is a database package which can be used to organize, store and retrieve research literature references. It saves precious time when writing-up and beyond. Using EndNote you can directly download references from online databases. As with all software packages, it is useful to work on this with someone who has used it before.

Reading the literature

Creating a table or template for recording what you have read can save both time and energy. Once again, the system you create must be personal to you. If you are an action researcher reading about action research carried out by other practitioners, you should take note of the following.

- What was the context of their research?
- Who was involved? Was it an individual or a collaborative project?
- Was the choice of using action research as a method justified? Are any models discussed?
- How were the data analysed?
- Were any ethical considerations addressed? How was this done?
- What 'actions' actually took place?
- How were data gathered, analysed and validated?
- What were the conclusions? Were they justified using appropriate evidence?
- Was the report accessible or useful?
- Is it possible to replicate this study?

Reviewing and writing up the literature

Always bear in mind what the purposes of reviewing and writing up the literature are. There is no one single way to do these, but here are some guidelines:

- It will be worthwhile to see how other researchers involved in similar projects – small-scale, Master's or doctoral level – have written up the literature review in their reports, theses or published papers. But it is also important to develop a personal style of presentation which suits your context.
- Start producing summaries of what you have read, starting with an overview of what the research topic is about. Organize these summaries under sub-headings

as themes. Under each sub-heading, give an account of the research undertaken, highlighting any findings. It is important not just to write a list of who said or found out what, but to also review the findings with an accompanying personal, critical commentary. It is also useful to highlight (perhaps in different colours) authors with similar views and findings as well as contrasting ones. There is nothing more tedious here, in my opinion, than reading a list of what each author said with no reflection on the contents or interconnecting commentaries.

- Time spent on the literature review is well spent, as it not only gives you more confidence in carrying out your research, it also saves time later when it comes to writing up your final report and any subsequent work on producing journal papers.

You could create a personal conceptual map, a visual summary (Creswell, 2009) of what you have read. Maps can be organized in different ways. You could place your research topic in the centre or at the top and link this with connecting arrows to boxes which record different themes and sub-themes and the names of authors and dates. This kind of map should help significantly when you write up your literature review.

Assume now that you have collected and read some literature which relates to your study. (At this stage, it may be useful to have a quick look at Chapter 7, where I discuss how you may present the literature review in your final report.) Remind yourself that an important purpose of searching for different sources of literature and reviewing them is to help you construct a framework for understanding the issues relating to your topic of investigation. This is done most effectively if you can relate the coherent story that emerges from your reading.

During one of our detailed discussions at the university on how to write a literature review, my students designed a format which you may find useful. They proposed a three-stage plan as follows.

i.   Identify the significant themes that have emerged from your reading. These would have been highlighted through written summaries and colour-coded sections while you were gathering and reading the literature.
ii. Introduce the ideas by themes rather than by listing different authors' viewpoints. If you write in sequence what others have said it can become very tedious and disjointed for the reader.
iii. Introduce each theme and explain what that particular theme is. Then present the evidence from your readings, both agreements and disagreements between experts. For example, if you are discussing the theme of using portfolios as a means to raise student achievement, explain what the particular theme means in this context and put forward the views of authors and experts on that theme followed by a critical commentary of what you think.

In this context Blaxter et al's (1996: 115) guidance to researchers on writing critical reviews of literature is worthy of consideration. The suggestion is that you use your references to:

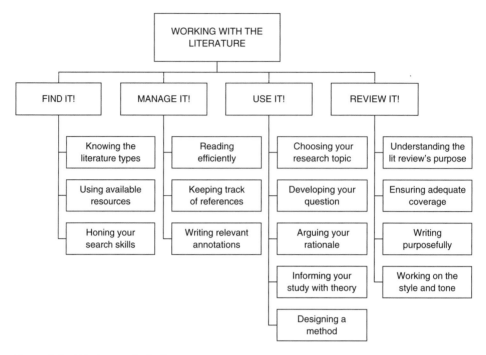

Figure 3.4   Working with the literature

- justify and support your arguments;
- allow you to make comparisons with other research;
- explain matters better than you could have done;
- explain your familiarity with your field of research.

O'Leary's representation in Figure 3.4 above provides an effective diagrammatic model of how the research process is supported by a literature search and its use. I will exemplify this model through the work of one of my students, Claire.

Case Study 📁

For Claire, the spark of interest in her topic was provided when she read the results of a survey which claimed that the examination marks of students who had attended problem-solving sessions improved by 24 points in mathematics and 22 points in science. Claire became interested in the topic of problem solving, but at this stage it just stayed as an interest for quite some time. Then, after a staff meeting which discussed the different ways boys and girls approached open-ended work, she decided to search for literature to find out more about problem solving. She read a range of books, including textbooks. She searched websites and came across a new set of resources on problem solving, produced as exemplars by a government agency.

(Continued)

(Continued)

It was a coincidence that at that time she was considering studying for a module on action research at the local higher education institution, and this gave her the context for carrying out a further investigation into the topic of problem solving.

Developing a research question

Claire knew that her topic of study could be related to problem solving, but at this stage she needed more knowledge about the topic. More searches and reading a range of literature around the topic helped her to identify an area for action research. She decided to study how boys and girls approached problem solving.

Articulating a context

The original rationale for the research question was her personal interest in the topic. Then further reading directed her to research findings which suggested that boys scored higher marks in problem solving than girls. She decided to design an intervention programme for problem solving and monitor the outcomes to find out whether there were differences in the performance of boys and girls when they solved problems. Her own studies also provided considerable impetus to her motivation to carry out a structured, small-scale investigation.

Informing your study with theory

It was time for more reading. Claire tracked down more readings – both theoretical texts and existing research literature – on three subjects which related to her research topic: *gender, achievement and problem solving*. Informed by all three sets of readings she was able to proceed with her action research project with more confidence.

Designing the method

Claire decided to carry out an action research project which gave her the flexibility to refine her activities as a result of evaluating and reflecting at each stage of her work. With a complex topic involving several strands to the exploration, the issue of flexibility was reassuring for her. Reading and analysing the literature also informed her about possible ways to collect data. For example, she realized that she needed to establish a base-line so that comparisons of pre- and post-intervention results could be made.

Writing up a literature review

Claire made systematic notes on the key issues discussed in the books and papers she read. She developed the themes she had identified within the literature and made critical comments on different issues. This process not only helped her to feel more well-informed about the topic of her study, but she also felt more prepared when writing up her final report at the end of the project.

 **Summary**

After the first step of making a start with action research as described in Chapter 2, this chapter explained the purpose of undertaking literature reviews and led you through the process of searching for relevant literature. Guidance was given on how to structure the search, evaluate Internet sources and organize the literature. Three kinds of literature were specified relating to policy, theory and related research publications. It was also proposed that a fledgling researcher should take note of the research methods used by others and critically appraise their findings. In this chapter I have attempted to suggest ways in which action researchers can forge their way through the literature maze.

 Further Reading

Cohen, L., Manion, L. and Morrison, K. (2007) *Research Methods in Education* (6th edn). London: RoutledgeFalmer.

Creswell, J.W. (2009) *Research Design: Qualitative, Quantitative, and Mixed Methods Approaches.* Thousand Oaks, CA: SAGE.

Hart, C. (2001) *Doing a Literature Search: A Comprehensive Guide for the Social Sciences.* London: SAGE/The Open University.

Merriam, S.B. (1998) *Qualitative Research and Case study Applications in Education.* San Francisco, CA: Jossey-Bass.

O' Dochartaigh, N. (2007) *Internet Research Skills.* London: SAGE.

O'Leary, Z. (2004) *The Essential Guide to Doing Research.* London: SAGE.

 Useful websites

- American Educational Research Association – http://www.aera.net
- British Educational Research Association – http://www.bera.ac.uk
- EPPI centre – www.eppi.ioe.ac.uk/cms
- ERIC – www.eric.ed.gov/
- SAGE's community for researchers from all disciplines – http://www.method space.com

4
Planning action

This chapter focuses on:

- making preparations and planning for action;
- using examples of projects to exemplify the need for action planning;
- facilitating an action plan;
- what to do when things don't go according to plan.

The previous two chapters focused on the various kinds of preparation that action researchers make before implementing action. You are now at the stage of having selected a topic and reflected on different aspects of that topic. You have undertaken a literature search and have done some reading which has enriched your understanding of different issues relating to the topic. As a result of your reading and further thinking, you may have changed or fine-tuned your topic of investigation. Now it is time for action. In this chapter, I will address many of the practical issues of carrying out action research, drawing on both personal experiences of supervising practitioner-researchers in different settings and from reading and hearing about action research projects carried out by other practitioners.

Carrying out action research is a rewarding experience. But a good action research project does not happen by accident; it needs careful planning, a flexibility of approach and continuous reflection on the part of the researcher. Although action research does not have to go through a pre-determined set of steps, it is useful here for you to be aware of the progression which I presented in Chapter 2. The sequence of activities I suggested then could be looked on as a checklist for you to consider before planning the practical aspects of your project.

So, here are some questions for you when you are about to begin.

- Have you identified a topic for study?
- Have you set a context for the study? (It may be a personal project for you or for a group of researchers of which you are a member.)
- Have you read some of the relevant literature?
- Have you designed your research question?
- Have you assessed the resource implications?

Before you start your project, it is worth writing down:

- a working title for your project which you may need to refine later;
- the background of the study, both in terms of your professional context and personal motivation;
- the aims of the project;
- the specific outcomes you are hoping for.

Although most of the models of action research presented in Chapter 1 suggest action taking place in some pre-defined order, they also allow us the possibility of refining our ideas and action in the light of our experiences and reflections. Changes may need to be made in response to your evaluation and your reflections on how the project is progressing. For example, you might have to make adjustments, taking into account the children's responses, your observations and any observations of your colleagues. All this is very useful and, in fact, it is one of the features that makes action research suitable for practitioner research.

Making preparations

Here is a practical activity for you to try. Read the following case study of a project which was written as a report for the funding body which sponsored it. The format is not the focus of your task, as I am sure it could have been presented in a different way. Read the case study and construct a detailed list of actions which could have been planned in advance. Your list can also include any preparations. You may find it helpful to annotate the text in pencil while reading it. Then compare it with the actual 'To do list' made by the researchers which I have included later on.

Case Study 📂

Title of project: Can we improve students' performance and achievement in mathematics by introducing a problem-solving approach to teaching?

Background

Our school is for 11–18 year olds and is located in an inner-city area which draws its pupils from predominantly lower income families. In recent years the mathematics achievement of pupils has been low. The new Head of Department in mathematics suggested that teachers for the first year intake in the school (12 year old students) organize an intervention programme in teaching specific problem-solving skills as a way of improving achievement. The school was successful in obtaining a small grant from a local business to enable a group of teachers to set up an intervention and undertake an action research project. A mathematics lecturer from a local teacher-training

(Continued)

(Continued)

institution was recruited to provide guidance with research methodology, especially with data collection and analysis which the teachers felt they needed help with.

Initial observations

During the preparatory stage, the group of action researchers observed their students' responses and made notes. Students' strategies for tackling mathematics work were noted. Their written work was analysed. Based on the initial data it was noted that most of the students were quite comfortable in producing correct answers to routine work, such as the four operations on numbers, including fractions and decimals. Students' strategies were based on the rote-learning of rules, as the interviews with students had suggested. This was also obvious when they were given word problems and investigations. The majority of students were unable to solve problems which involved multi-steps and they lacked confidence in even making a start with investigational work. The researchers discussed the issues they had to address and formulated an action plan. An analysis of the school's syllabus and the requirements of national mathematics tests suggested that students needed problem-solving skills and processes to tackle their mathematics work more effectively. The project was set up.

Intervention

Preparations for the intervention programme started with an extensive literature search on problem solving. The researchers sought to find all recent and relevant literature on problem solving and its possible influence on mathematics learning. Resources on problem solving, mainly consisting of tasks with detailed notes and justifications for their use, were purchased. After four weeks of discussion and deliberation the four teacher-researchers selected 20 activities to be used in mathematics sessions over two terms (six months). They met once a fortnight to share their perceptions and the data gathered from the sessions. The information collected was also shared with two other mathematics tutors and the local mathematics adviser who acted as Critical Friends. Some changes were made to the type of resources used and the times of the session as a result of discussions.

Data collection

Data collection was discussed with the supervisor from the university. The following sets of data were collected:

- a short questionnaire before the intervention started with four questions seeking students' attitudes to mathematics, their views of their own abilities and their perception of what mathematics was all about;

(Continued)

(Continued)

- a pre-test consisting of questions testing both routine and problem-solving tasks;
- researchers' logs to record significant incidents and events during the problem-solving sessions – comments on individual students were to be included;
- a post-programme questionnaire using the same questionnaire issued prior to the start of the programme;
- a post-test using similar items to those used in the pre-test.

All the data were analysed collectively by the four teachers. The findings were shared with the group of Critical Friends, the Head of the mathematics department and the university tutor. A workshop was planned to disseminate the findings of the project.

The findings

At the start of the project:

- pupil participation in mathematics sessions was minimal in terms of discussion;
- their contribution increased at a very slow pace;
- students' views of mathematics showed that they perceived the subject as useful and as consisting of sums;
- the intervention programme increased students' participation in discussions;
- increased confidence was recorded in the case of approximately 25 per cent of the students;
- students made a quicker start with problem-solving situations, compared to their pre-project reluctance and disinterest;
- there was an increase in the mathematics scores of 23 per cent of students.

Researcher's views

- Researchers felt that a longer period of intervention may have produced better results in terms of increased confidence and achievement.
- Lower ability students made more progress; this trend was the same across the four classes. This aspect needed further investigation and analysis.
- The researchers felt that they needed to further analyse the content and processes presented through the commercially produced problem-solving materials. They revised their teaching methods in response to their evaluation of the level of improvement in the students' attitudes and test results.
- The match between the skills and the process, as required for the tests and teachers' current teaching methods, needed further investigation.
- There was a noticeable shortage of recent research literature on problem solving within the UK.
- The participant researchers felt that they were greatly enriched through their experience. The sustained collaborative work and reflection, they believed, were necessary ingredients for their professional development.
- When the results of the research project were published, the researchers received a large amount of correspondence from colleagues in the profession, who asked for more details of the project and for help in setting up similar projects in their geographical areas.

I hope you have compiled your own 'action list', including the necessary preparations that you need to make prior to the start of the project described above. Now compare your list with that list constructed by the researchers, who actually carried out the work, which is given below. The purpose of this exercise is perhaps self-evident. I am trying to highlight the importance of planning in advance and anticipating the outcomes and difficulties when you are carrying out action research.

The 'To do' list for the problem-solving project and related notes is as follows.

- Evidence of lower achievement in mathematics. Where does it come from? Who says so? How reliable is the source? Compared to what? Collect and compare school results with the results nationally, in the local education authority and neighbouring schools.
- What are specific problem-solving skills? Find out. Look at documents and analyse national tests. Ask your university tutor to suggest readings. Do a web search for ideas and published papers.
- Make a list of the specific aims of the project.
- Draw up a time-scale.
- Get the ethical procedures sorted out. Let parents and children know about the project.
- Set up a validation group and willing Critical Friends and make sure they know their roles.
- Establish what data are needed and what may be feasible.
- Discuss an observation schedule and establish the guidelines for consistency between researchers' observations.
- Organize dates for meetings – of researchers, with colleagues, the validation group, Critical Friends and your university supervisor.
- Create a filing system for storing the children's written work.
- Think about video recording sessions.
- Order problem-solving resources (check with your local mathematics adviser).
- Design pre- and post-questionnaires and pilot these first.
- Organize your pre-tests.
- Discuss the format of researchers' personal logs.
- Consider your data analysis.
- Think about your dissemination of the project. List some ideas.

Although I would acknowledge that action lists are always personal to a researcher or to a group of researchers, there are some features of the above list which do make it a useful model for you to consider. Here are my reasons.

- The list is comprehensive and gives attention to detail. The time spent on planning activities is worthwhile, as it will help with the smooth running of the project.
- The researchers understand the need for establishing a set of specific aims.
- The plan is very detailed and pays attention to practical aspects, such as the storing of students' work and decisions relating to possible formats for researchers' personal logs.

- The researchers acknowledge the need for enhancing their own understanding of the topic of study. For example, they aim to seek further clarification of what is meant by problem-solving skills and plan to consult documents and search for relevant readings.
- The need for a base-line is highlighted at the outset.
- The researchers intend to involve others – colleagues, the local adviser, the university tutor and Critical Friends – to provide feedback.
- They consider what data are needed as evidence, to be collected in advance.
- It is quite a good idea to consider the dissemination of outcomes at the outset, as this helps you decide what to collect and store, as well as the nature of the evidence required.
- Let the participating students and parents know about the project and give them the choice of whether to participate. This is an ethical issue, which is discussed in Chapter 5.

Facilitating an action plan

The role of a supporting mentor or supervisor is of vital importance to an action researcher. In the following section, I have presented a few short transcripts of some of my tutorials with a Master's student. Ian is a secondary school teacher who was studying for a Master's degree. After completing all the required taught modules, he was preparing to carry out research for his dissertation. Although he subsequently finished his dissertation, which was of a very high quality, in the initial stages he was quite uncertain about what he was doing and how he could manage it all. As part of my preparations for writing this book, I asked Ian if I could tape-record our tutorial sessions and he kindly agreed. The purpose of including these transcripts is to reinforce the ideas I have highlighted earlier in this chapter. Ian maintained that the tutorials helped him to focus on his topic and the methodology. You may perhaps identify with Ian's experiences, which should encourage you to reflect on some of the issues I have discussed earlier. I acknowledge my gratitude to Ian for letting me tape-record our conversations and allowing me to share these through this book. With the help of these transcripts, I have tried to highlight the stages which an action researcher or group of researchers may go through. Supervisors of research projects may also recognize these exchanges with their students.

Tutorial I

During this tutorial the following conversation took place.

Ian: I am at the stage of starting to think about my dissertation. I have just a vague idea what I want to do. That is it really, I haven't thought about it any further. All I know for certain is that I need to get the work done in six months and write up within four months after that.

VK: What is the topic you are interested in?

Ian: Something on questioning skills.

VK: What about questioning skills? Tell me more.

Ian: Well, I got interested after our assessment lecture on differentiation. Bloom's taxonomy had an impact on my thinking. It is great. I want to do something relating to that as my topic.

VK: What aspect of Bloom's taxonomy interested you the most?

Ian: I was rather hoping you would tell me what to do and how to do it.

VK: Let us start again. You said you were fascinated by the taxonomy, so you tell me what made you so interested.

Ian: The clarity of how the degree of cognitive demand increases when you move on to the higher levels.

VK: Yes, go on.

Ian: I also thought it is a great framework for a teacher to follow. I am sure most of us use the first few levels of the taxonomy in our teaching and never move onto the higher levels of thinking.

VK: Is that one of the areas that impressed you? Tell me more.

Ian: Yes, I think I will do my project based on the application of Bloom's taxonomy in my lesson planning with reference to questioning.

VK: Now you have an idea to develop, the next step is …

Ian: What I would really like you to do, if that is OK, is for you to give me one or two tasks to do before I see you again.

VK: Well, how about these tasks. Try and write down a working title for your project, it does not have to be final. Second, write half a page of A4, explaining why you wish to undertake the study. You can include an explanation of how you got interested and what motivated you. The third task – write down what Bloom's taxonomy means to you, in your own words.

Tutorial 2

Ian sent me his attempts at the tasks before our next tutorial. During the second tutorial we discussed different directions for the study and Ian decided to select the title: 'Applying Bloom's taxonomy in my teaching'.

After more discussions, Ian decided on a different title: 'An investigation into possible changes in children's responses, when they are asked questions from the higher levels of Bloom's taxonomy'. Ian explained his 'hunch that children's answers to questions which test knowledge or comprehension will be quite brief and the questions which involve analysis and evaluation will be fuller and possibly more interesting and demonstrate more challenge in their thinking. Ian had brought a box file, which contained his lecture notes on Bloom's taxonomy and abstracts of two research papers on the topic. During our discussion we decided he needed to read more about his topic and do a web search for any international studies which investigated similar ideas to his. He was asked to bring his thoughts to the next tutorial along with an action plan.

I also encouraged Ian to look at some studies of other Master's students in the library which had been bound and were on display.

During the next tutorial Ian said he was happier with his new, focused title and brought an action plan which included the following.

Ian's list

- Read three research papers and the lecture notes again before deciding on the nature of the questions to be used.
- Read about action research as a methodology and jot down why I have selected this as a method to conduct the study. (See notes from research methods lecture.) Include a reference to the participatory nature of action research.
- Focus on three lessons in a week. Possibly from one single subject so that other variables are not introduced.
- Write down a set of questions from the different levels of the taxonomy in the lesson plans.
- Arrange video taping one session per week for six weeks. Think about what else can be collected as evidence.
- Organize two colleagues to watch the video and make independent comments.
- Make any necessary changes after three weeks.
- Create a time-scale for the fieldwork.

The purpose of including an account of what transpired during tutorials is to highlight a few issues which could be useful to those readers who may feel some anxiety at the start of their project. It is quite common for new researchers to select a topic based on a new experience or a new idea which has raised their interest. It is likely that the initial title would reflect a wish to take on the topic in its entirety – remember, this may be unrealistic and unmanageable. On many occasions you may have only a vague idea about your research topic, but there is no need to feel guilty about that. Most of my students find it very useful to talk their ideas through with their supervisors and also with colleagues in teaching sessions. Many of them also appreciate being given structured tasks between tutorials. An example of a research planning grid I use with prospective action researchers is presented below. This systematic process helps them to reflect on their plans and subsequently revise these as necessary. The different chapters of this book would certainly guide you in completing the grid. When completed, this could provide a basis for discussions between supervisors and students, as well as between fellow researchers.

Action research planning sheet

I have included the comments that I provide to my students in the grid (in italics) and I then ask them to complete a *blank grid of their own.*

My topic of research is about …	*At this stage, you may only have a general idea about the area of study. Writing it down will help. For example, in Ian's case he wrote 'improving my questioning skills'.*
Why do you wish to research this topic?	*There could be different reasons for this. Perhaps you read or heard something about the topic? Ian's choice was influenced by a lecture on assessment using Bloom's taxonomy and the levels of cognitive challenge in questioning.* *Professional reasons may be important here, such as a new responsibility within your institution or attending a professional development course, or it may be that your institution has applied for funding to undertake an action research project. It could also be that you realized you need to improve/change something in your practice.*
Are your plans workable?	*What possible challenges might you face? A lack of time? Colleagues may not hold the same views as you and could perhaps block the progress of your project. Make a list.*
Write down a working title. What is your research question or aspect you are intending to study? What do you know about your topic of study?	*This may take several attempts. From all your ideas, select the most elegant and focused title which conveys your intentions clearly.* *Your initial knowledge about the topic can be recorded here. Ian wrote what he knew about the levels of thinking and how these were formulated and where they came from. What readings and literature are available that you know of? A conceptual map may help.*
Where will I search for literature? Who will be involved in the research? What is the time-line? What ethical procedures do you need to put in place?	*Chapter 3 will give you plenty of guidance for this. List everyone who will be involved: colleagues, children, parents, external evaluators. Construct a realistic time-line. State briefly what arrangements will need to be made for ethical clearance.*
What data do you need to collect? Why do you need each of them? Having completed the grid so far, do you need to change anything in your plan? Make a list and record the reasons. This is an important stage in all research activities.	*Make a list of the kind of data you need and next to it justify why you need to collect them and what methods you intend to use.*
What are the possible outcomes of my research?	*List the possible benefits and outcomes for you, personally and professionally, for the people you teach or work with, and for your institution. You may also think about what knowledge may be generated that could be shared with others.*
What is your research question?	*You may have changed it after completing the previous sections of this grid and if not, you still need to write down what the research question is. Good luck with your project!*

Figure 4.1   Action research planning sheet

When things go wrong

As in the case of most plans we formulate, and even after making every effort possible, things can go wrong at any stage of the research. Just to highlight a few of these: some parents may not give permission for their children to take part in the research project; parents whose children are not participating in the project may feel that their children are being left out; parents may need to be reassured that the project's findings which are judged to be effective will be implemented in the classroom for all children. Students may also move from the area or be absent for long periods of time which can create problems if your investigations involve a small group. Or your action plans and data collection may not always go according to plan. Perhaps your Critical Friends will suggest that data collection methods are flawed or too subjective and you may have to start all over again, which could challenge the validity of your findings. You may run into financial problems. Or some of the problems that arise may be due to conflicts with colleagues who may not subscribe to the ideas you are trying out. You need to anticipate all of this and therefore various consultations and conversations need to take place prior to the start of your project. Many of the organizational and resource related problems can be avoided, if you antic-ipate them during the planning stage.

Having discussed the importance of forward planning and attention to detail, it is time for you to think a little more about what I have discussed previ-ously. The case report below is designed to facilitate your further consideration of the issues of action planning which were discussed earlier.

Here is a different task. Have a look at the title of the Case Study below (*title only at this stage*) and make a note of what planning needs to be done before the start of your project (doing this with colleagues will generate useful discussion). Only after making your list and notes, should you read your report.

Example

Developing the speaking skills of pupils for whom English is an Additional Language (EAL) through playing board games

Aims

- To design a set of board games which will encourage children to engage in more speaking.
- To investigate whether teachers can improve the speaking skills of Year 2 children (6 years old) for whom English is an Additional Language (EAL pupils), by engaging them in specially designed board games.

What was the study about?

This study investigated the effects of using specially designed board games on the development of speaking skills in 16 pupils in a class over a six-month period. The

(Continued)

(Continued)

research was carried out by the literacy coordinator with support from the local education authority's literacy consultant and the local adviser for children for whom English is an Additional Language.

Summary of findings

- In most cases (11 out of 16) pupils showed considerable improvement in their speaking skills as a result of playing specially designed board games.
- Initially, pupils were reluctant to participate in the board games. They felt that their lack of ability to speak fluently would be a barrier to winning these games.
- The quality of children's talk improved during the intervention programme.
- The project provided opportunities for involving parents and carers in the development of the children's spoken language.
- Parents who were involved in the project commented that their own language skills had improved as a result of the project and they felt better able to support their children's learning at home.

Background

This research project was located in a multicultural infant school with 212 pupils. For 63 per cent of the children English was an Additional Language. The aim of the study was to raise the children's achievement. In this particular project the development of children's speaking skills was targeted, as it was hypothesized that their lack of such skills could affect their writing skills. The children who participated in the project were all well behaved but seemed to lack confidence in participating in class discussions. This lack of confidence may have been the result of their inability to speak English fluently. An intervention programme using games was planned for two reasons. First, children are generally quite motivated to participate in such games and, second, playing board games would involve working in groups, thus generating the need to talk as a means of communication.

Specific objectives

The project was set up to:

- investigate what contributes to the development of speaking skills – this would be achieved through reading literature and by consultations with experts;
- establish the level of speaking skills among EAL children prior to the project – this would provide a basis for monitoring;
- design a set of ten board games, which would encourage use of the English language;
- encourage children's parents to participate in the project by sending copies of the board games home, with instructions in both English and the language spoken at home;
- monitor any changes in the children's development of vocabulary, their fluency of speech, their reading skills and their level of confidence;

(Continued)

(Continued)

- assess whether the programme would have any effect on the children's writing skills;
- disseminate the findings and ideas for the resources to colleagues and other local schools.

Gathering data

A number of methods was used. The project was set within a qualitative paradigm. As it involved a small sample, the use of quantitative data could not be justified. However, evidence of changes in scores was recorded numerically. The following information was collected:

- baseline test results;
- samples of children's writing throughout the period of the project;
- tape recordings of group activity throughout the project to gauge the level of participation;
- a researcher's diary of significant events;
- copies of board games and a list of anticipated learning outcomes resulting from their use;
- pupil attendance.

Design of the board games

The board games were designed by a researcher, taking into account research findings on the development of speaking skills. The support staff actually created these. Instructions were word-processed. Multiple copies of both the games and their instructions were made available for children to take home.

The intervention programme

Parents were informed of the project before the start. Children were involved in the games session four times a week for approximately one hour. At each session, data were collected by the researcher and validated through discussions with colleagues and local advisers.

Results

- There was an increased level of confidence in the children's speaking skills as evidenced by their readiness to talk and the spontaneity of their responses. Indicators of increased participation were also noted. Children's reluctance to go outside at playtime, so that they could continue to play the games, was quite common.
- The number of English words used in the session increased steadily throughout the period of the project.
- Parents also showed a high level of commitment to the programme. They were actively involved and very enthusiastic for their children to bring the games for homework and they always *played* with their children. One parent commented on the board games taking over from *television time*.

(Continued)

(Continued)

- There was a marked improvement in the quality of the children's writing (this was independently verified by colleagues).
- There was, however, no marked improvement in the children's reading skills. The research team was invited by a national publisher to help develop a set of board games in both mathematics and English, specifically designed for EAL children.

Endnote

The project was worthwhile in terms of the enhancement of children's literacy skills, and speaking skills in particular. As there was no control group, it could not be claimed without qualification that it was the intervention programme that produced such positive results. Using a control group was beyond the scope of this project. One certain, beneficial aspect of the project was the learning processes it offered to the researcher. At the start of the programme, the researcher was frustrated and helpless and wishing to take some positive steps towards helping her EAL children to participate more in the lessons. The outcome of the project was pleasing in that it achieved its aims. The researcher's own knowledge of teaching EAL children was enhanced through her own reading and by her 'living' the project over a sustained period.

Reading this detailed case study and comparing your list of what planning was needed should highlight the importance of the attention to detail required at the preparation stage.

Here is another useful scenario for you to read and consider. It is possible that you may be involved in making a funding application for carrying out an action research project. The account below contains extracts from a successful proposal requesting funding, by a group of teachers from neighbouring schools, to carry out an action research project. See what you think.

Example

Can the use of Information and Communications Technology (ICT) encourage students to develop effective learning strategies?

Aim of the proposed project

To establish whether focused training in the use of ICT can help students to develop effective learning strategies.

Background

All students in Year 7 at our schools (12 year olds) will carry out a personal research project. The aim of such a the project is to develop students as researchers. The learning strategies we wish to develop in students are skills of research, critical thinking,

(Continued)

(Continued)

meta-cognition, reflection, analysis, evaluation and making effective presentations. We also wish to develop students' awareness of bias and enhance their awareness of ethical issues. Carrying out a personal research project has the potential to develop all the above skills listed; we believe that training students in the use of ICT will enhance the development of these skills to a much higher degree.

We have carried out an extensive literature research on the role of ICT training in developing students as effective researchers/learners. One of the findings we have identified from our literature search is the increased motivation of students who had received training in ICT which had also led to higher achievement. We wish to set up this project to assess the effectiveness of ICT training with regard to students' acquisition and enhancement of the skills listed above.

Research plan

We wish to set up the proposed project, using action research as our methodology. Action research would enable us to plan activities and make modifications as the research progresses. We believe that action research is a suitable methodology for this project as it involves practitioners from several schools working together on a practical aspect of our working lives. The knowledge we generate would contribute to our professional development and we intend to share our findings through networks of professional organizations and writing up the outcomes for publication in professional journals.

We are teachers from two mixed gender schools, two single sex girls' schools and two single sex boys' schools, all situated in the same education district. We will work with our own classes and the British Education Research Association code of Ethics regarding research involving students will be followed throughout. At present all classes of 12 year olds carry out a personal research project. The intervention ICT training, as part of the preparation of students' research projects, will be provided for our own classes of students (ranging from 25 to 29 students). The parallel classes which will not receive the ICT training until the following year will serve as a comparison group. The intervention will be for a period of five months.

The intervention

The ICT training intervention will include an Internet search for information, the design and completion of questionnaires on line, data analysis using software packages (Excel, for example), the setting up of group e-mails, word processing and training in the use of Powerpoint. Research skills will be taught alongside ICT training sessions.

Data gathering and interpretation

In order to assess the effectiveness of the intervention, the following data collection techniques will be deployed. Data will be collected from both the intervention groups and comparator groups and comparisons will be made.

(Continued)

(Continued)

- Interviews with a sample of students about their feelings and experiences regarding ICT training and the perceived impact of the training on their learning.
- Observations of students working on their research project and their making use of ICT skills. We will triangulate the data for greater validity and trustworthiness.
- Students' work will be collected to assess whether the use of ICT enhances the development of skills identified at the start of the project. DVDs which capture students at work will be produced, including their final presentation of projects to an audience including parents.
- Analysis will initially involve the generation of rich description of pupils' experiences and their perceptions of impact. Qualitative data will be analysed using coding techniques.

Project management

A validation group will be set up to read and comment on all the data collected.

The project group will meet weekly to discuss progress and any possible modifications. A research officer will manage the project on a day-to-day basis. There will be continuous contact between the researchers and the research officer.

Anticipated outcomes

For students in the intervention group

- Students' level of ICT skills will be greater.
- They will demonstrate a greater level of skills for research, critical thinking, identifying bias, meta-cognition, reflection, analysis and evaluation.
- Students' literature search skills will be enhanced which, in turn, will add to their knowledge base on the subject of their personal research.
- Students will demonstrate greater skills in data collection and analysis.
- Presentation skills will be enhanced and demonstrated in all the students' work as a result of the training provided.
- Students would experience increased motivation in carrying out research projects.

For teachers

- Greater understanding and practice of ICT skills.
- Opportunities to work collaboratively to encourage student learning.
- Experience in action research methodology: planning, action, data gathering – analysis and interpretation, evaluation and reflection.

Relevance and significance of the findings

The outcomes of this project will add to the knowledge base on the use of ICT to develop research skills and more effective learning strategies. This is an area which has not been researched with the age group in the proposed project. We intend to disseminate the findings of the project and artifacts at both professional association and research conferences. The final report of the project and the resources we create will be made available to colleagues nationally.

 **Summary**

In this chapter I have stressed the importance of drawing up action plans. The construction of a 'To do list' of action followed. The role of Critical Friends and colleagues was emphasized, as I believe that the dynamics of collective thinking can create an awareness of any shortcomings as well as generate previously unexpected lines of enquiry. Case studies are provided as guided tours via journeys taken by other action researchers. These were presented to enable readers to acquire a kind of simulated experience of action research before embarking on their own, real journey of enquiry.

 Further Reading

Baumfield, V., Hall, E. and Wall, K. (2008) *Action Research in the Classroom.* London: SAGE.

Hopkins, D. (2002) *A Teacher's Guide to Classroom Research*, 3rd edition. Buckingham: Open University Press.

O'Leary, Z. (2004) *The Essential Guide to Doing Research.* London: SAGE.

McNiff, J. and Whitehead, J. (2005) *All You Need To Know About Action Research.* London: SAGE.

Taber, K. (2008) *Classroom-based Research and Evidence-based Practice: A guide for Teachers.* London: SAGE.

 Useful websites

- www.triangle.co.uk
- Action Research – www.actionresearch.net
  - An academic journal which publishes studies of interest to action researchers.
- The Collaborative Action Research Network – www.did.stu.mmu.ac.uk/carn
  - Provides details of research publications and research conferences.
- *Educational Action Research* – www.tandf.co.uk/journals/titles
  - Gives details of the above journal.

5
Gathering data

This chapter focuses on:

- aspects of methodology;
- ethical considerations;
- methods of data collection and the relative advantages and limitations of these;
- the use of case studies as an approach.

When you set up an action plan for your action research, you will have given some consideration to an all important part of conducting any research – gathering data. You would probably have been asking yourself one particular question for some time: what methods will I be using and how will I go about organizing the collection of data? If you are working towards a qualification you would also have been attending lectures in your academic institution on research methodology. This chapter is devoted to aspects relating to data-gathering. As I mentioned in Chapter 4, as preparation for writing this book I kept tape-recordings of some of my tutorials with students and practitioners who wished to adopt action research as the methodology for their research. I start this chapter with a transcript of one such conversation. Martina, study-ing on a Master's programme, was intending to carry out a project on curricu-lum differentiation. After the first few tutorials, she decided to narrow the focus of her study to investigating how three class teachers of 10 year old children in her school addressed curriculum differentiation in their classrooms and then considering what changes they might implement to improve their practice.

Our conversation

Martina: I am now ready to start collecting data. I have got some ideas. First, my worry is that I am only working with just three teachers. Is that a big enough sample?

VK: Big enough sample for what?

Martina: Big enough to have any credibility when I write it up.

VK: Why do you have such doubt?

Martina: I thought you had to collect information from a larger sample for any research.

VK: Let us go back a bit. What is the purpose of your research – of course, other than the fact that it is part of your study? What are your aims?

Martina: To find out how different teachers deal with differentiation and learn from it. I will compare what I find out from other classrooms with what happens in my classroom. I need to think carefully about what I am doing. I need to evaluate our practices by asking questions and reflecting on what is happening. That will guide me to generate practical ideas to achieve better curriculum differentiation for a second cycle of work because my head teacher wants me to design a policy on classroom differentiation based on our research.

We then talked about the timescale that Martina had to complete the project, in terms of the requirements set by her school and her study for accreditation purposes. We also discussed the nature of action research which, in Martina's case, would be a small-scale project and a focused study on aspects of practice. Action research offers opportunities for asking 'What is happening here?' and 'How can I improve my practice?' We agreed that the purpose of her research was not to make any generalisations about curriculum differentiation for the whole country, but to study a snapshot of what was happening in her school with a small number of the teachers involved. Personal theorizing of principles through participatory research was the main purpose of Martina undertaking her study. We then went on to discuss what kinds of data she needed to collect.

In the following sections I will present a variety of data-gathering methods, together with their relative merits and any possible disadvantages for their use in action research. The ultimate decision of what kind of data you need and what methods to use will depend on:

- the nature of the evidence you need to collect;
- the time-scale for the study;
- the time available to you for carrying out the project;
- the usefulness of the data you intend to collect;
- a consideration of how you may interpret the data.

The number of different methods you intend to use for collecting data does not make your study any better; indeed I would say that it is the quality of the data you collect that matters. A set of data which has no depth is not going to prove useful when the time comes for data analysis and drawing conclusions. Keep reminding yourself that you will need to analyse the data you collect and provide supporting evidence from that data to justify your conclusions.

Your reading would have provided you with some insights into what aspects you will be looking for. In Martina's case, she decided use a range of methods of data collection: interviewing class teachers on their perceptions of how they achieved differentiation in lessons; collecting lesson plans from all the teachers involved; observing their lessons and collecting students' written work. Martina was encouraged to consider some of the aspects she would be looking for and also how she needed to allow for unexpected outcomes. Running a pilot study was also suggested to her so that she could consider how she was going to organize her data. She and I discussed when she was going to collect her data and looked into the practical aspects of school time-tables and cover. Did she need to prepare any special resources? What ethical considerations needed to be built into the process of her data collection? Did she have permission from the teachers she was going to study? Had she considered how she was going to share her perceptions and observations with the three other teachers participating? Martina also decided to ask two of her colleagues, who were teaching a different year group, to act as Critical Friends.

Discussion of methodology

Before considering what data-gathering methods to select, it is necessary to revisit the discussion we had previously on the philosophical underpinning in the context of action research, in terms of its ontological and epistemological considerations. Ontology is concerned with the beliefs we hold about what we are enquiring about. Epistemology – our theory of knowledge – is concerned with our beliefs about what it is possible to know; whether we believe that 'absolute truth' can ever be known. It is important for you to voice your philosophical position as your research design, data collection and analysis will be influenced by your beliefs. If you are carrying out your research as part of obtaining a qualification, you will certainly need to demonstrate some knowledge of different research paradigms. An elaborate discussion of different paradigms of research is beyond the scope of this book, so if your study is leading to a dissertation you will need to do some supplementary reading which would be provided in your research methods lectures and from what is listed at the end of this chapter.

Researchers often refer to *positivist* and *naturalistic* paradigms. A positivist (see the glossary of key terms) researcher often gathers large amounts of data in the form of large-scale surveys and analyses them in order to make generalisations, while a naturalistic, interpretative researcher tries to get inside individuals and institutions to understand situations and people. As an action researcher whose research is bound to be located within your specific context that generates knowledge relating to that specific situation, you are likely to follow an interpretive paradigm.

Quantitative and qualitative data

Action researchers should also be aware of the two categories of data – quantitative and qualitative – and consider their usefulness within the context of their work. Quantitative data can be measured and represented by numbers. When a researcher handles large amounts of data – for example, a large number of questionnaires, surveys, or tests results – it is often necessary to analyse these using statistical methods and presenting them in the form of tables and charts. If you are collecting views by using questionnaires from a small group of children or colleagues about their perceptions of a style of teaching or attitudes, you may want to represent the data numerically using such tables and charts. The use of questionnaires within a qualitative study often provides ideas for further exploration. However, it is likely that an action researcher would predominantly be working within a qualitative paradigm as the data may be more in the form of transcripts, descriptions and documents for analysis. It must be stressed that qualitative data are not inferior in status and, in action research, that it can illuminate human feelings and provide rich insights into actions and their consequences. What is important is to select the type of data which will best serve the purpose of your study. If you are undertaking action research for the purpose of obtaining a qualification, it is well worth including the distinction between quantitative and qualitative paradigms in your writing-up in order to demonstrate your understanding of research methodology and to provide a justification for the methods you have selected for data collection. Creswell (2009) defines qualitative research as a means of exploring and understanding the meaning individuals or groups ascribe to a social or human problem. The process of research involves emerging questions and procedures, data typically collected in the participant's setting, data analysed inductively building from particular to general themes, and the researcher making interpretations of the meaning of the data. In this context, you may remember the view of *social constructivism*, as discussed in Chapter 1. Creswell (2009) maintains that 'social constructivists hold assumptions that individuals seek understanding of the world in which they live and work', that they 'develop subjective meanings of their experiences' and that the goal of the research 'is to rely as much as possible on the participants' views of the situations being studied'. As a result, action researchers who are seeking to generate 'living knowledge' (Reason and Bradbury, 2001) could be described as 'social constructivists'.

Cohen et al's (2007: 166) justification of the use of qualitative methods also provides support for the action researcher in educational contexts. They state that 'the social and educational world is a messy place, full of contradictions, richness, complexity, connectedness, conjunctions and disjunctions. It is multi-layered, and not easily susceptible to the atomization process inherent in much numerical research'. The following features of naturalistic enquiry which is qualitative in nature – listed by the authors – also justify the use of an interpretive methodology for action research.

- Humans actively construct their own meanings of situations.
- Meaning arises out of social situations and is handled through interpretive processes.
- Behaviour and thereby data are socially situated, context-related, context-dependent and context-rich. To understand a situation, researchers need to understand the context because situations affect behaviour and perspectives and vice versa.
- Realities are multiple, constructed and holistic.
- Knower and known are interactive and inseparable.
- Generalisability is interpreted as generalisability to identifiable, specific settings and subjects rather than universally.

An action researcher may use a variety of methods to collect data. Ask yourself the following questions before you start collecting your data.

- What are the aims of my research?
- What aspects am I focusing on?
- What do I need as evidence to achieve my aims?
- What is realistic and feasible?
- How should I record the data?
- How would I analyse the data?

Ethical considerations

When you are carrying out research it is important to follow ethical guidelines. Academic institutions should maintain a set of guidelines for their students to follow. Reading the guidelines on ethics published by the British Education Research Association (BERA – see the section on useful websites at the end of this chapter) is a useful starting point. Following strict guidelines on ethical issues is of particular importance for action researchers because of the small-scale nature of the projects located within the working situations of such researchers. Special care needs to be taken both for data collection and the dissemination of findings as it would be easy to recognize people and events within local situations.

I would add a special word here about research involving children, which is often the case within action research. You will need to seek permission from the children who are to be involved in your research and not just from their parents. In line with the (1989) United Nations Convention on the Rights of the Child (and see the website at the end of this chapter), you must explain to the children what their role is in the research and that they will be free to drop out of this research at any time during the project.

- Always obtain permission from the participants. If you are collecting data about children, their parents need to be informed. The same principle applies to colleagues, members of local education authorities, parents and governors.
- Provide a copy of your set of ethical guidelines to the participants.
- Explain the purpose of the research. In action research the outcomes are most likely to be used for improving aspects of practice and, therefore, there is less likelihood of resistance from participants.
- Keep real names and the identities of subjects confidential and unrecognizable.
- Share information with colleagues and others whose responses you are interpreting so they can verify the relevancy and accuracy of what you are reporting.
- If you are intending to introduce new ideas and set up interventions with pupils, their parents need to be told.
- Be sensitive to the feelings and perceptions of both parents and students. This is particularly important if the intervention programme is designed to

improve aspects of education, as the students being targeted may be seen to be at an advantage. You need to make it clear that the findings of a research experiment will benefit all.

- Be as non-intrusive as possible in your data collection.
- The information you gather and the changes you make as a result of your research should be shared with all the particpants – both adults and children.
- When you are researching socially sensitive issues, you need to make an extra effort to share your purpose and objectives with the participants.

A checklist before you start your data collection

You may find the following checklist useful before you start collecting information for your project.

- Are any ethical issues being considered?
- Have you got permission from all those who will be involved in the project, such as parents, colleagues and the head teacher?
- Have you checked all the equipment you will need to use? Are the tape recorders, video recorders and cameras operable?
- Have you considered how you will validate the information for accuracy, trustworthiness and relevance (see Chapter 6)?
- Where and how will you store the information?
- Have you a general idea as to how you can analyse and interpret the data (see Chapter 6)?
- Have you organized the resources you need, including any costs?

Methods of data collection

In the following section, we will look at methods for data collection which are commonly used within action research. Data collection methods are also referred to as methods of instrumentation. Before exploring the different methods, let me provide you with two important points which all researchers could usefully bear in mind when planning their data collection.

- There are many ways of gathering data; you have to choose the most suitable method for the task in hand.
- The quality of the data you collect is more important than the number of ways you collect that data.

The methods described in the following sections are:

- using questionnaires;
- conducting interviews;
- gathering documentary evidence;

- keeping field diaries and making notes;
- using systematic observation.

For each method of data-gathering, I have tried to provide some general guidance as well as indicate various advantages and any possible disadvantages for that particular method. Some examples are given in those sections that I felt needed exemplification.

Gathering data questionnaires and surveys

Using questionnaires at the start of a project can often be very useful because it helps you to collect a range of information with relative ease which can then be followed up as necessary. For example, if you are carrying out a study on how an intervention programme may help to change student attitudes towards learning a particular subject, use of a questionnaire will provide you with a simple means to collect information on student attitudes, before any intervention takes place. The completed questionnaires can help in two ways. Firstly, they provide baseline data on student attitudes before the intervention begins. Secondly, an analysis of the questionnaires may help to shape the nature of the questions you may want to ask during any interviews or observations you might conduct. Within a questionnaire, you can use both short questions and open-ended questions which need fuller responses. When working with children, I often find they enjoy the experience of completing the questionnaires so they can be encouraged to provide full information in response to questions. It is possible to set up questionnaires on-line and experience shows that students do prefer to complete these as opposed to pencil and paper versions.

Guidelines

Here is a set of guidelines you should find useful to consider.

- Keep the questionnaire simple. By designing appropriate questions, you can often gather a decent amount of data using a small number of questions.
- Consider how you may analyse the responses to the questions at the time of their design.
- Start with questions about the factual information required.
- Use simple language which the respondents will understand.
- Closed questions asking students to select their favourite lesson in school, from a given list (English, mathematics, science, humanities and technology) are easier to analyse by using a frequency chart. Open-ended questions, for example asking students what career they thought they would follow when they leave school, had posed a real challenge to our research assistant at the time of analysis. This question generated so many different responses – including 'I haven't thought about it', 'I don't really know yet' and 'Nothing, I will win

some money by then' – that this made the analysis much more complex. Some items had to be clustered together for that analysis to take place. But the responses to these question often captured 'real' situations and feelings which proved very illuminating for the researchers, who were also constructing student trajectory maps of changes in their aspirations and attitudes.

- Open-ended questions are useful, but do give some thought as to how you would analyse them.
- Avoid leading questions. For example, a question such as 'Which part of the lesson did you enjoy the most?' assumes that the student enjoyed some parts of a lesson, which may not necessarily be the case.
- Emphasize the anonymity of the responses, as children and adults are often sensitive to who else may be told about how they have responded.
- Undertake a pilot run before you give out your questionnaires and make any adjustments as necessary. In your final report acknowledge your pilot effort and any changes that were made for the final version of the questionnaire.
- Questions do not always have to use words. For example, I have seen some effective use of pictures of happy, puzzled or sad faces, with younger children being asked to select a picture in response to questions such as: 'How do you feel when you are asked to answer a mental mathematics question during a carpet session?'
- Take account of the reading ability of students when administering a questionnaire.

Advantages of using questionnaires

Questionnaires

- enable you to collect background and baseline information quite easily;
- provide information which can be followed up;
- provide a format which is easy to represent in frequencies if you wish to use them;
- are suitable for collecting initial information on attitudes and perceptions.

Disadvantages of using questionnaires

- You may be subjective and introduce bias in the type of questions you ask.
- Responses to questions may be influenced by what the respondents believe you want to hear.
- Designing a questionnaire needs great skill, especially when you use open-ended questions which are designed to be probing. Take note of the previous section about the challenges involving an analysis of open-ended questions.
- If you are using questionnaires in order to collect data from a large group of people who are not within your institution, returns and response rates may be too low to ensure a valid research outcome.

An example of a questionnaire

As part of her data-gathering activities, Stephanie, a member of the senior management team in her school, decided to use a questionnaire to collect information about students' interests, aptitudes and aspirations, prior to designing an intervention programme to be delivered after school to bright students who had the potential to go to university. This was part of a new government initiative. The extracts in Figure 5.1 are taken from Stephanie's questionnaire.

Students' responses to the questionnaire proved useful to Stephanie. Her own evaluation of the use of the questionnaire was as follows:

Example

I used about ten multiple choice questions at the start, which the students could respond to quite quickly. As there were about 120 students taking part in the project I was pleased to be able to collect a good amount of information without much effort. The analysis was simple, as I could classify the responses into numbers and represent them visually, using tables and graphs. I felt that the open-ended questions were necessary to encourage students to reveal their aspirations and expectations without giving them predetermined options to choose from.

Responses to the open-ended questions involved greater effort when it came to analysing them. Nevertheless, these questions provided answers relating to some of the aspects I needed to explore. I needed to find out the kinds of aspirations the students had and their perceptions of how they would be able to achieve them. Analysis of these types of questions revealed some significant information. For example, only 14 students expressed any desire to pursue an academic career and listed university education in their future plans. It was also very useful to note that a large number of students had dreams about becoming successful pop singers or sports personalities. In general, the questionnaire provided much useful data which helped me to design an intervention programme that needed to include some strategies to introduce realism in students' aspirations (without shattering their teenage dreams). I selected a sub-sample of students to interview in order to gather more information. I did refine the questions after a pilot run, but it was worth the effort because the questionnaires enabled me to collect much useful data within a short time.

You may consider using Likert scales (where respondents mark on a strongly agree, disagree, no opinion, agree and strongly agree scale) which are also easier to analyse numerically (see Further Reading at the end of this chapter).

Conducting interviews

The main purpose of conducting interviews is to gather responses which are richer and more informative than questionnaire data. In some cases, adults and children will give more honest responses in a one-to-one situation. As it is

The purpose of this questionnaire is to help you to think about any interests which you may like to pursue or develop. It will also help me to organize some out-of-school activities for you. The information you give in the questionnaire is confidential and will not be shared with anyone else, unless you wish me to do so. For some of the questions you are asked to provide brief answers and, for other questions, you are invited to give more information.

1. **Imagine you are one of a group of students who won a prize in school to set up an exhibition. What role would you want to take?**

    A. Organizer
    B. Artist
    C. Writing and designing brochures for publicity
    D. In charge of sound effects
    E. Any other (say which, and explain why):

        ....
        ....
        ....

2. **Suppose a publisher approached you and asked you to help an author write a students' book on one of the following subjects. Which of these will you choose?**

    A. Science
    B. Mathematics
    C. History
    D. Social issues
    E. Art
    F. Technology
    G. Other:

        ....
        ....
        ....

3. **If you could select from the following club activities after school, which would you choose?**

    A. A sports activity
    B. Creative writing
    C. Learn a new language
    D. Web design
    E. Learn to play a new instrument
    F. A different club activity that you would like to see in the list. Say which:

        ....
        ....
        ....

4. **What do you expect to be doing in ten years' time?**

    ....
    ....
    ....

5. **What do you think you should do between now and ten years' time to achieve what you want to be?**

    ....
    ....
    ....

Figure 5.1   Questionnaire example

impossible to take notes on all that is said during an interview I recommend tape-recording the interview, if the numbers are manageable. You can make the choice of whether you listen to the tapes or read fully transcribed versions of the interviews when you wish to analyse them. Tape-recording also makes it possible for the researcher to give full attention to the context of the interview.

Interviews may be conducted with individual students or in a group and there are different kinds of interviews. In a **structured interview** the interviewer starts with a set of questions which are pre-determined and only these questions are asked. In a **semi-structured interview**, the researcher prepares a set of questions but also prepares a set of sub-questions which can be used to probe ideas further and gather more information. There is also the option of using **open-ended interviews**. In an intervention programme for raising (13 year old) students' motivation and achievement, a teacher researcher used the following open-ended questions.

- Why do you think you go to school?
- What do you like or dislike about school?
- Can you describe a good experience you have had in school?

Students were encouraged to provide full answers to these questions. The interpretations themselves were different in different cases, but that in itself provided useful data. If you decide to conduct group interviews using open-ended questions you should really get a set of different responses, although there is always the danger of students copying each other or some students trying to dominate the discussions.

There are also other kinds of interviews such as focus group and telephone interviews (see Further Reading at the end of this chapter).

Some guidelines

- Select comfortable surroundings for the interview.
- Make sure that the interviews are not too long. About half an hour to 40 minutes for each is about right.
- Have some idea about what you want to ask. This will, of course, depend on the research topic and what aspects you are investigating. Semi-structured interviews allow you to probe further during the interview.
- If you intend to ask factual questions start with them.
- Begin with a simple question.
- Explain the purpose of the interview in a positive way. I often start with: 'I need your help to find out more about ...' or 'I am working on a project to write something about how children ... and what you are going to tell me will certainly help'.
- Assure interviewees' anonymity so that they feel relaxed.
- Try not to convey your opinions at the interview.
- Avoid leading questions such as: 'When I asked you what 5 and 5 makes, did you use your fingers?', 'Spellings are easy for you, are they not?'
- Open-ended questions can often provide you with richer information. Some ways of encouraging children to talk more is by using phrases such as 'That

is interesting', 'Tell me more' and 'How would you explain that to someone who does not know anything about it?'
- Sometimes it is fruitful to interview a group of children together. It is very important to keep children focused during group interviews.
- Always review the responses to interviews and refine your procedures and questions if necessary.

Advantages of carrying out interviews

- Interview transcripts provide powerful evidence when you are presenting your data and making conclusions.
- Interviews can provide a relaxed context for exploration.
- Information from interviews can supplement what has been gathered through questionnaires and surveys.
- The interviewer can steer the discussion through a fruitful route.
- Group interviews save time and are realistic in classroom contexts.
- Interviews can often provide unexpected but useful perspectives.

Disadvantages

- Conducting interviews is more time-consuming than using questionnaires.
- Typing transcripts requires a significant amount of time.
- Interviewing may not always be a suitable method to use with children who are not confident speakers and those with language problems.
- Tape recorders may intimidate some students.
- The interviewer's presence may make interviewees nervous and bias any responses.
- Children may tell you what they think what you want to hear.

A sample interview

Stephanie, whose questionnaire was discussed in the previous section, interviewed a sub-sample of students after they completed their questionnaires. The following interview with Guli was revealing.

Stephanie: I see you have written here that you would like to see yourself as working in the City earning a lot of money. Tell me more about it.
Guli: I mean a lawyer or something like that. They earn a lot of money and do an interesting job.
S: What would you find interesting about a lawyer's job?
G: All sorts of things. Now let me think ... [pause]
S: No rush, do think about it before you tell me ...
G: I like watching lawyers on television. They have to really think hard about how to argue a case even when they know their clients are guilty. That takes some work. I also like the way they have to stand up and argue point by point. It looks as though they are really enjoying their job.

S:	Anything else that appeals to you?
G:	Yes, they all dress so smart and have posh cars.
S:	Do you think you will become a lawyer?
G:	I would like to, but it is hard. My mum wouldn't know how to go about it. You would have to go to university, won't you? My mum can't spell the word university let alone send me to one ...

The second transcript is an interview with Lloyd.

Stephanie:	You have said you want to earn a million pounds as a footballer. Do you think you will make it?
Lloyd:	It is a dream really. It doesn't matter if it happens or not, does it?
S:	I am just interested to know how you would go about achieving your dream. For example, tell me why you think you could become a successful footballer.
L:	Because I want to be one.
S:	Do you play football?
L:	A bit on Saturdays.
S:	Would you say you are good at football?
L:	I am all right. I suppose you are thinking ... [pause] ... you are thinking ... I am not good enough to become a rich footballer. I suppose you will be right. Only very few people can really become millionaire footballers ... There is no harm in dreaming though ...

Stephanie wrote about her interviews:

It really was very revealing. Guli is a very bright girl, but I had no idea that she and her family would need support to consider an academic route for her. There were other students I interviewed who also showed similar needs. I am happy to say that this information helped me in two ways. First, it highlighted the need for organizing some parents' sessions in which to talk to them about career choices and educational require- ments; this could become part of my intervention programme. It also provided a baseline for Guli at the start of the programme which enabled me to track her progress. In Lloyd's case, it occurred to me that even during my interview he started questioning the nature of his ambition and viewed it as an impossibility. It made me think that as part of our intervention programme it would be useful for students to be encouraged to think about the feasibility of their ambitions.

Gathering documentary evidence

In some cases your data collection would include studying documentary evidence such as policies, minutes of meetings, teachers' planning records and students' work to supplement other data sources. These sources can often provide a useful background and context for the project and can also be very illuminating, especially when you are comparing what is claimed and what has happened in practice. One of my students, looking for evidence on differentiation, found several claims about differentiation in the school policy, but little evidence of it in practice within curriculum plans or in the actual teaching which she observed. Documents can often provide relevant evidence and are very useful for constructing the whole picture. I have seen students using curriculum planning records over a period of time and keeping an ongoing record of any changes. Similarly, students' written work and portfolios can help researchers to note progress over time. Photographs capturing critical moments and products are also useful as evidence. This is particularly helpful in Early Years' classrooms. Students' journals can provide an excellent set of information to show evidence of the level of student engagement in the activities, the development of processes such as reasoning, critical analysis and so on. Although the documents can be very illuminating, you do need to be selective in what you keep. One way of organizing the collection of documentary evidence is to design a table and list the documents on the left-hand side and what information each document is likely to provide you with. Decide that you will only keep key documents which are directly useful for your research.

Advantages of gathering documentary evidence

- Documentary evidence can provide insights into a situation where research takes place.
- In most cases it provides information without too much effort.
- A record of objectives and policies which are not easily communicated can be accessed through documents.
- It can support other forms of evidence collected.

Disadvantages

- Trust in the researcher will be necessary before access to documents is given.
- As it may constitute large amounts of data, selection and analysis could be difficult.
- Personal choices may affect the type of documents collected.

Field diaries and notes

Use of a research diary, or field notes as they are sometime referred to, is often very helpful and this device is becoming more popular with my students. It is adopted to keep a record of what happens, of why and where your ideas evolved and of the research process itself. It is a place where you would keep an account of your reflections and write a personal commentary on your feelings as well as the beginnings of your interpretations. Your research diary could be extremely valuable when it comes to writing up your project as it contains your authentic voice as described during the research process. The reflective process involved in writing a diary contributes to the professional development of researchers. Diary entries need not be very long. You could record significant events during your observations or particular situations and your feelings.

Guidelines

- A free writing style can be employed when keeping field notes and diaries.
- It is useful to have a structure in your mind. Within that structure, you need to have the flexibility to make notes about aspects which may not fit into your predetermined structure, although these are significant to you.
- Reflective writing supports professional development. Try to be analytical and reflective in your entries.
- Including a section for personal commentary which supports analysis and discussion at a later stage.

Advantages of keeping research diaries

- Keeping a research diary helps to personalize your project. This is important in an action research project as the main purpose is to make changes in practice.
- Diaries help to keep a progress check on the project.
- Field diaries often supplement information obtained from other sources.
- The process of reflective writing is an integral part of your professional development.
- The contents of a diary should help you to construct your research story as a case study.

Disadvantages

It is difficult to think of any disadvantages in keeping a personal journal of incidents during an action research project. However, the following aspects may be worth considering:

- A researcher may be tempted to write too much, which can lead to difficulties at the time of analysis.
- It is sometimes difficult to maintain your writing regularly.
- When your research is not going according to plan, there may be a tendency to stop writing.
- Personalizing incidents may lead to a level of subjectivity.

Systematic observation

Observation plays an important part in any kind of data-gathering and most action research projects use this as an instrument. Observation is a natural process – we observe people and incidents all the time and, based on those observations, we will make judgements. Basically, we are making use of this method within the research process where there is a need for more systematic observation, so that the information we collect can be used for the purpose of the study being carried out.

When we consider observation as a method for data collection, two types of observation are often referred to – participant and non-participant observation. *Participant observation* involves the researcher living in the context and being a part of it, but one needs to be aware of what Cohen and Manion (1994) point out – that there is a danger of being too subjective in data collection and this can introduce bias. One also needs to be conscious of this and acknowledge, at the outset, the possibility of introducing into the data gathered what one wishes to see. We must also try not to distort the interpretations. *Non-participant observation* is less subjective. This involves observing actions and interactions, perhaps sitting in a corner of the room, silent but attentive. Both types of observation require a careful planning structure.

Structuring observations

The nature and purpose of the observation process will influence the level of structuring we need to introduce. Through structured observations, we can gather both qualitative and quantitative data. Using carefully designed checklists or observation schedules, we can record behaviour patterns and the number of actions and interactions. In semi-structured observation procedures one may still use checklists and schedules, but some flexibility is required to record both comments and unexpected outcomes. In action research, I feel that the flexibility of recording unexpected outcomes is of some value.

Contexts for observation

Let us now consider some contexts in which an action researcher may make use of observation as a method of data-gathering.

Observing colleagues
If your project involves observing colleagues you will need to have some dialogue with them to discuss both organizational issues and the principles you would want to follow during the observations. For example, you need to make some decisions about where, how often and how long the observations

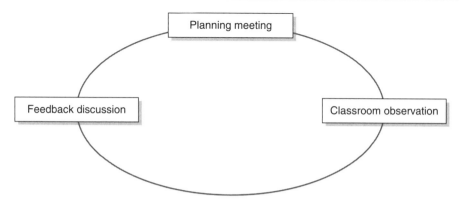

Figure 5.2   The three-phase observation cycle

will be. You must study any schedules and checklists and establish a common understanding of what you are observing. It is also advisable to discuss how you will share your observations with the observed and what form of feedback will be given. This kind of discussion will help to build up trust and make the whole process more effective. An example of this would be when you decide to research the teaching styles of a group of teachers. A researcher completing checklists and making notes would observe each of the colleagues. In this context you would have established, prior to the observation, what you propose to observe and record and how you would validate your observations. When you are observing colleagues, consideration should also be given to your approach. You need to show sensitivity and be unobtrusive. Any feedback should be non-judgemental and relate to the criteria established between you and those you observe.

The three-phase observation cycle proposed by Hopkins (2002), shown in Figure 5.2, is worthy of consideration.

There are three essential phases in Hopkins's model. The *planning meeting* provides the observer and the teacher with an opportunity to reflect on a proposed lesson, which then leads to a mutual decision to collect observational data on an aspect of the teacher's own practice. During the *classroom observation* phase, the observer observes the teacher in the classroom and collects objective data on an aspect of teaching they have agreed upon earlier. During the *feedback session* the observer and the teacher share the information gathered during the observation, decide on appropriate action, agree a record of the discussion and then plan another round of observation.

Here is an example of an observation of a colleague by another colleague. The project title of the action research project was 'Who does the talking?' The project involved two teachers who decided to observe each other to establish the level of teacher talk in the classroom. The objective was to try to increase student participation and discussion and the starting point for this was to make an assessment of one's teaching style at the start of the project. Helen and Matthew, two colleagues, had an initial meeting to select a lesson for observation and studied the lesson plans. They decided that Helen would sit at the back of the classroom and make notes on the amount of time Matthew spent talking to the students and also the length of time his pupils were involved in responding and discussing. She would make a note of the nature of the questions he asked as they both felt that to be relevant. Helen drew a plan of the classroom and the seating arrangements as they felt these too would have some impact on the level of pupils' involvement in the lesson. It was decided that Matthew would explain to his class that Helen was observing him in connection with her own studies, as he felt that being told the objective of the observation may encourage students to change their behaviour for that session, thus defeating the purpose of the activity.

After a lesson was observed, Helen and Matthew met and discussed Helen's notes and perceptions. They also discussed the possibility that the nature of a question may partly affect pupils' talk. They decided to change the nature of some questions and planned another observation.

Here it can clearly be seen how the observation process fits well into the action research model, which involves selecting a topic, planning, collecting data and taking action based on the findings.

Observing pupils

The process described above may not be suitable if you are observing pupils. It is not always possible to plan and discuss your ideas with pupils, especially if they are younger. Having said that, some of my students had to tell their pupils why they were writing things down when the pupils became curious and wanted to know why they were making notes about them. To reduce the disruption, children were told that their teachers were making notes to help them to think about how their teaching could be made better.

One example of student observation involved watching a group of pupils who were referred to as *disruptive* to identify patterns in their behaviour such as the context, the nature of the lesson and the teacher input during the times in which any disruptive behaviour occurred. For this exercise Carole, an Early Years teacher, decided to involve a colleague in carrying out an open-ended observation of selected children using no preconceived plans or checklists.

The notes from the observer on Nadia, 4 years and 6 months, looked like this.

9.00 Nadia sits down at the front of the carpet; she is completely still.
9.04 Teacher greets the students and asks them what they had been doing over the weekend. Nadia, with a few others, puts her hand up.
9.06 Teacher selects Nathan to tell the class what he had been doing during the weekend.
9.12 Nadia gets up and goes to the front of the class, sits down and holds the teacher's hand. She then gets up again and goes to the choosing corner.

9.13 Teacher asks Nadia to come back to the carpet, which she does not do.
9.15 Teacher says, 'Come and tell us what you have been doing over the weekend'.
9.19 Nadia runs back to the carpet and enthusiastically talks about her visit to see a donkey ...

Guidelines

- Decide whether you are going to be a participant or non-participant observer. When you wish to observe while you are working with a group of children, it can be difficult to be a non-participant observer.
- Consider access and timescales for your observations.
- Quite often a structured observation schedule is useful; this may be an established structure or one that you must design for the purpose in hand.
- If you are using a predetermined checklist, you may want to record unexpected outcomes which could be of significance within the context of your project.
- Think about your analysis while preparing your observation schedules. Remember, you will need to analyse your data soon afterwards.
- Consider how you will validate your observations.
- Try a pilot observation and refine the process as necessary.
- Make a note of any difficulties you encounter; these may be of significance when you come to analyse your data and write up your report.

Advantages of observation

- Open-ended observations allow you to capture all aspects of the topic of study.
- It offers first-hand data.
- You need to collect information through a systematic observation and recording of what you see and hear.
- It offers a way of studying, through a close scrutiny of behaviour. Observations provide you with opportunities to make a note of reactions (boredom, frustration and disinterest, for example) which are also of value in the construction of your narrative.

Disadvantages

- Too much information may be collected which could pose a challenge at the time of analysis. Selecting what to observe during observation may become difficult.
- Being observed may affect the behaviour of the person observed.
- Organizational problems may stand in the way.

- Background noise and disruptions may lead to missing important data.
- There may be a temptation to skip over details if they do not fit with the items on a pre-prepared checklist of what to observe.

Using video and DVD recording and photographs

Using videos and DVDs to record events is becoming increasingly popular as a data-gathering technique. The availability of digital cameras and other technological resources has made recording a viable and effective way of gathering information. One of the advantages of video recording is that it allows the researcher to observe an activity afterwards by watching the video, without the disruptions of the classroom or time constraints. By viewing recordings, practitioners can analyse different aspects of the activity as well as identify an unexpected point which may be significant. These recordings are also very useful when it comes to collecting accurate information on student participation and attitudes. For recording critical incidents in the classroom a digital camera can provide both photographs and a few minutes of video/DVD recordings.

Advantages of video/DVD recording

- Student behaviours and attitudes can be captured with greater accuracy than by making observation notes.
- Provides a more permanent record of incidents, which can be viewed and reviewed.
- Makes sharing data with colleagues and fellow researchers easier to manage.
- Very useful at the time of dissemination. Recording provides powerful images which are hard to match through other means of communication.
- It makes it possible to carry out studies which need a sustained period of development and data collection so as to note changes.
- Video and film clips can often generate a good deal of discussion between observers and audiences with whom you will be sharing your findings.

Disadvantages

- Being recorded can be inhibiting and distracting for the participants.
- Those who are being recorded may behave differently in the presence of a camera.
- The usual technical hitches may lose useful first-hand data which cannot be replaced.
- Photographs may be selected according to the photographer's perception of the importance and significance of incidents.

An example of using a recording for an action research project

Jill was carrying out an action research project on the impact of introducing a Critical Thinking programme to her 13 year old students, in terms of raising student achievement and enhancing their level of confidence and listening skills. Jill chose a range of methods to collect evidence for her project. She felt she could track changes in students' achievement in terms of test scores and by collecting tangible examples of their work in a range of subjects over a period of time. She also felt that data on any possible changes in the level of students' participation in the programme, their confidence and listening skills were more effectively gathered through video recordings over a period of time.

Jill wrote in her report:

> My project was to explore whether the introduction of a structured Critical Thinking programme would help to raise my students' achievement in different subjects. Another objective of the study was to note any changes in students' confidence in taking part in discussions. I felt it was straightforward to compare the results using tests, but collecting evidence on changes in students' level of confidence and participation was rather more challenging. I needed something visual, which could be looked at over a period of time. Using video recordings provided me with an opportunity to achieve this. After every session which I recorded, I watched the recording and asked myself 'What is happening here?', 'Is there any change in the students' behaviour?' If there was, I asked myself what may have contributed to the changes. I showed the recordings to my colleagues who independently reviewed the sessions and made comments. I kept a reflective diary of what I thought was happening. I identified where my objectives of the lessons matched the outcomes in terms of students' responses to the sessions and attitudes. At the time of dissemination at the local teachers' centre, I showed sections of a video recording to illustrate students' behaviour over a period of six months. Data in the form of video recordings offered me authentic evidence to convince other people of the impact of my project.

Quality indicators

Action research is a unique approach in carrying out enquiries into aspects of practice. Although the purpose of action research makes it different from large-scale research studies which use surveys and questionnaires, the action researcher still needs to consider questions of validity, reliability and generalisability within the context of the particular research study. I discuss these in greater detail in Chapter 6.

First, we need to consider the **validity** of the data. This means we need to consider the accuracy of what is collected and used as evidence. We have to be aware that the conclusions are based on the quality of what we gather as data. Interpretations of the same event or evidence can vary between different people. This can affect the validity of the data presented. One way of establishing validity, according to Mason (2002: 246), is to find 'various means of confirmation, such as arranging for a colleague to observe as well, arranging for audio or video recordings, and asking other participants for their versions'. Mason recommends *triangulation* for this purpose, which he describes as the process of obtaining several viewpoints or perspectives. The word '*triangulation*', he explains, is based on the method of surveying land which breaks the region down into triangles, each of which is measured. Hopkins (2002: 133) also emphasizes the role of triangulation in data-gathering, 'as it involves contrasting perceptions of one actor in a specific situation against other actors in the same situation. By doing so, an initial subjective observation or perception is fleshed out and gives a degree of authenticity'. Hopkins quotes Elliot and Adelman (1976: 74) to describe the process of triangulation, which is useful for an action researcher to consider:

> Triangulation involves gathering accounts of a teaching situation from three quite different points of view; namely those of the teacher, his pupils and participant observer. Who in the 'triangle' gathers the accounts, how they are elicited, and who compares them, depends largely on the context.

The authors justify the process of gathering accounts from three distinct standpoints in terms of the three points of a triangle having a unique epistemological position.

In the context of action research we also need to consider the aspect of *reliability*. Reliability is described as the consistency or stability of a measure (Robson, 2002) and a consideration of whether, if the measure is repeated, one would obtain the same result. Hopkins (2002) makes a useful distinction between validity, which reflects the internal consistency of one's research, and reliability, which reflects the generalisability of one's findings. He maintains that, in general, most action researchers and those who use qualitative methods are concerned with validity rather than reliability, in so far as their focus is on a particular case rather than a sample.

In the case of practitioner research, the researcher needs to emphasize that generalisability is still possible, in terms of the project being applicable to other similar situations and, in some cases, the study's replicability.

Use of case studies

Carrying out case studies is a popular approach used for studying settings within qualitative methodology. It is a qualitative study which looks closely at what happens, collecting data, analysing information and presenting the results as accurately as possible. Case studies can be focused on one single case or on multiple cases. They offer rich descriptive data and considerable depth. One of the advantages of presenting a case study is that the reader can often identify with the case and the characters in the case study.

Yin (2003) describes the case study as a research strategy with an empirical enquiry that investigates a contemporary phenomenon within its real life context, when the boundaries between phenomenon and context are not clearly evident, and in which multiple sources are used. This description of a case study resonates well with the processes involved in action research. Case studies, as in the case of action research, are sometimes criticized for the inevitable subjectivity involved in creating a narrative, but this subjectivity is reduced by sharing the data with those who are involved in the study.

In terms of analysis, carrying out case studies provides us with opportunities to explore both the *how* and the *why* of events (Yin, 2003) and these can be both exploratory and descriptive. Detailed descriptions of cases allow the reader to engage in situations and apply findings within their own context – again, you can see how case study methodology sits well within an action research approach.

Many action research projects are written up as case studies. The following advantages of a case study outlined by Adelman et al. (1976) support their use as a means of disseminating action research projects. The authors' description of case studies demonstrates why they are a powerful means of capturing real data which can act as a basis for action.

- The data within a case study are strong in reality but susceptible to ready organization.
- This strength in reality arises because case studies are down to earth and can hold the attention, in harmony with the reader's own experience, and provide a natural basis for generalisation.

See Further Reading at the end of this chapter which will provide you with more information on how to conduct and write up case studies and about the different types of case study design.

☐ Summary

This chapter directed the reader's attention to issues of data collection. Large amounts of data, like literature, can be overwhelming in their abundance. Guidance on selection and pertinence was given and a distinction was made between quantitative and qualitative data. The merits of qualitative data for the purpose of action research were highlighted. The importance of addressing ethical issues was also stressed. Issues of validity, reliability and generalisability, within the context of action research, were discussed and the role of triangulation as a means of quality control was also raised. The advantage of using a case study approach within action research was also briefly addressed.

 **Further Reading**

Bell, J. (2005) *Doing your Research Project* (4th edition). Buckingham: Open University Press.

Cohen, L., Mannion, L. and Morrison, K. (2007) *Research Methods in Education* (6th edition). London: RoutledgeFalmer.

Drever, E. (1995) *Using Semi-structured Interviews in Small-scale Research: A Teacher's Guide*. Edinburgh: SCRE.

Flyvbjerg, B. (2006) 'Five misunderstandings about case study research', *Qualitative Inquiry*, 12: 219–45.

Hopkins, D. (2002) *A Teacher's Guide to Classroom Research* (3rd edition). Buckingham: Open University Press.

Kvale, S. and Brinkman. S. (2009) *Interviews: Learning the Craft of Qualitative Research Interviewing*. London: SAGE.

Silverman, D. (2004) *Doing Qualitative Research: A Practical Handbook* (2nd edition). London: SAGE.

Stake, R.E. (1995) *The Art of Case Study Research*. Thousand Oaks, CA: SAGE.

Wragg, E. (1994) *An Introduction to Classroom Observation*. Abingdon: Routledge.

Yin, R.K. (2003) *Case Study Research: Design and Methods* (3rd edition). Newbury Park, CA: SAGE.

 Useful websites

- AERA Ethical Standards document – http://www.aera.net/aboutaera/?id=222
- American Psychological Association – http://www.apa.org/ethics/code 2002.html
- British Educational Research Association – http://www.bera.ac.uk/publications/guides.php
- Unicef, Convention on the Rights of the Child – http://www.unicef.org/crc/

6

Analysing data and generating evidence

This chapter focuses on:

- organizing, analysing and representing data;
- a range of examples of data analysis;
- the role of computer software on data analysis;
- validating evidence;
- making claims and contributing to knowledge.

Your action research project is now entering a crucial stage. You have planned your project with meticulous attention and gathered data using different methods. Now it is time to carry out the final analysis and represent your data, prior to drawing conclusions and sharing your findings. While carrying out your action research project, with its cycle of planning–data-gathering–evaluating–acting, you will have been making some form of analysis of your data and now, at this final stage, you will be pulling together all your findings and reflecting on the implications of these findings for practice, as well as identifying unanswered questions and new directions. The time it takes to analyse and present the data may depend on the nature of the project. For example, for a researcher who is undertaking a study which is leading to an academic dissertation, the process of analysis may take longer as there would be a larger amount of data to organize and analyse. Many of my students experience mixed feelings at the analysis stage. After many months of work, they can feel quite excited about analysing the data before drawing conclusions, as it marks a significant stage in their research process. They can also feel quite overwhelmed by the amount of data they have collected and a little unsure about the final stage of data analysis. I think if you have collected your data carefully and addressed the issues of validity and reliability as you have progressed through the study, the analysis stage should not pose any real difficulties.

As an action researcher, you have to create a coherent and credible story from all the data collected. You may have used a mixed methodology and collected some quantitative and qualitative data, but it is more likely that most of your data are qualitative. If you have used qualitative methods for data collection the presentation of evidence may take the form of descriptions. I personally feel that analysing qualitative data is as challenging as analysing and presenting quantitative evidence. At this point, the action researcher also needs to be aware of some of the criticisms made, by many, that action research is a 'soft' option in which the practitioner researcher works with a small number of people and therefore this is not 'proper' research. To address this criticism, I would just reiterate what I have said previously – that an action researcher is involved in investigating a question or a topic within his or her own context, where the focus is on a single case or that of a small group of people. It is part of the professional development of those involved. An action researcher is looking to create meanings, using rich descriptions and narratives. An action researcher develops expertise through looking at situations closely and analysing them, recognizing any possible bias and interpreting data, rather than looking to generalize findings based on the study of a large numbers of cases.

Making a start

Before beginning your final stage of data analysis, it is important that you revisit the aims and expectations of the project. Think about what your research question or hypothesis was and remind yourself of what it is exactly that you have been investigating. I suggest to my students that they write all this on a card and place it in a prominent position while they are working with the data. During data analysis you are trying to identify themes and patterns in order to be able to present robust evidence for any claims you are about to make. You need to look at the data you have collected from several sources and relate these to what your original, expected, outcomes were. Of course, as with any good researcher, you would also be looking out for unexpected outcomes which may be of significance to report them too. Your conclusions must relate to the original aims and objectives of the project. It is also useful to remind yourselves of all the literature readings you have done during the project, which should in turn help you with the analysis.

At this stage of the research, it is important for you to reflect on the research process – from the initial stage of planning – and to make notes on how your proposed plan worked and about your experiences during that data collection. It is possible that most of your ideas and organization went according to plan, but you may have encountered unexpected problems and have had to solve them. As I discussed in Chapter 3, even with a best effort to make everything work out smoothly, things can still go wrong, as in educational establishments unexpected challenges do occur. Those who will be interested in reading about your research and possibly replicating it in their own settings will certainly be interested in knowing about the difficulties you experienced, as well as your successes.

Table 6.1   Details of data collection

Type of data	How was it collected?	How many?	Dates of collection
Questionnaires	Students completed these using computer	31	23rd September – 25th September
Interviews	One-to-one structured interviews		
Observations	Participant observation		
Student trajectories	Observation of attitudes and recording on a map		
Attendance			
Researchers' diaries			

Organizing your data

Although what follows may sound obvious, here is a useful suggestion. As you collect the data, make a note of everything you have collected and the numbers involved; for example, how many questionnaires you used, interviews you conducted, sessions you observed and students' learning trajectories you tracked. This helps you to keep focused on all the data sets. When you report your findings you may wish to present these in a table (see the example in Table 6.1), which will provide the reader with an overview of the whole data-gathering exercise and a clear picture of all the data sets.

The next step is to have a look at the notes or personal journal you have kept during your data collection. You may have been making some analysis of the data while you were collecting these. You could have been making personal notes on the themes which related to your original research aims, questions or hypothesis. As you were doing this you may have made decisions about whether you needed to gather additional data; make a note of this too. You might also have been making a note of any unanticipated themes or ideas that emerged and noted any shortcomings in your data collection methods. It is useful to remind yourself of these before you start on your final stage of data analysis and reporting.

In order to get started on a discussion of issues relating to data analysis, I have included three examples of action research projects in the following section. These were carried out in three contexts and the time frame in which these were carried out varied from three months to one year. These examples should provide us with some reference points and help us to consider choices in selecting appropriate ways of analysing and presenting data.

Examples of action research projects

Example

Action Research Project 1

Enhancing group discussion skills in a classroom with 5 to 6 year olds

Susannah, a class teacher of a group of 6 year olds, set up a small-scale action research project (three months of practical work in total) which aimed to enhance the discussion skills of her children. After reading around the topic and seeking external advice and support on how to carry out her study, she set out her data-gathering process as follows. She collected:

- Pre- and post-project interviews with the whole class of 23 children.
- Observation notes of lessons, every week, produced by the class teacher and a total of four observations by a colleague.

Before presenting her analysis of data, Susannah wrote the following:

> At the outset, I need to explain the difficulties I experienced in observing children. Being a participant observer created difficulties with observation. My presence during group work made the students talk less as they seemed to expect me to want them to work quietly. The data collected by my colleague as a non-participant observer provided more useful data.

The data were analysed in the following ways.

i. For both pre- and post-project interviews, students' perceptions of 'talking' in class were listed under different categories relating to the questions asked. Examples of the type of questions analysed were:

- When do you talk in lessons?
- When is talking in class useful?
- Does talking make work easier or harder?
- What does your teacher think of you talking in lessons?

ii. Detailed notes of lesson observations were given in the form of a narrative. Here is an extract:

> There were five children doing the activity – three boys and two girls. The activity was about guessing a 'mystery number' from clues written on a card which was also read out. 'Just one card with questions for all of us to share', muttered Ben. Asha looked disinterested and then looked in the direction of Melanie who was chatting away to everyone else, as she does during most of the activities. James and Stuart were talking from the start, but they were discussing a television programme and trying to work as a pair. Children were told that they could work together to find the answers to the mystery number questions. I was sitting nearby, but not participating. I had told the children they were not to come to me during this session because I was writing some notes for something I was doing for my own study. I observed the following:

(Continued)

(Continued)

> Melanie talked the most and directed all the discussions about strategies. Ben tried to work with Melanie but did not get much of a chance to say a lot. Asha was quiet, as always, but was paying attention. Two of the other boys, James and Stuart, started working as a pair.

Susannah kept on-going notes of her observations. The notes on the above session read as follows:

> It seemed that my expectation that one card with the questions will be sufficient for all five children was wrong. Ben articulated his concern straight away. Was I right in splitting Asha and Suresh (with Asha in the present group), who usually work together, just for this experiment? James and Stuart choosing to work as a pair, within the group, suggests to me that five was too large a number for that particular activity ...

In a subsequent observation Susannah tried a similar activity with four children instead of five and found that there was more interaction in that lesson. In her analysis of the observations she presented descriptions of what occurred in each of the group sessions and how her own strategies for group work changed the frequency and nature of the children's discussions.

Example

Action Research Project 2

An intervention programme to increase children's understanding of place value

Valerie, a Year 4 teacher (9 year olds), undertook this project requiring six months of fieldwork for her Master's dissertation. She felt that an enhanced understanding of the principle that our number system is based on the value of a digit being determined by the position it occupies within a number is central to children's number work, so that an increased understanding of this principle would reduce their mistakes and help their mental arithmetic work.

Valerie's project aimed to set up an intervention programme which was designed to help her class of 21 children acquire a greater understanding of the place-value concept.

During the project, Valerie collected the following types of data:

- a pre- and post-test on mental arithmetic questions and written number operations, with the whole class;
- interviews with a smaller number of children, at pre- and post-project stages, asking them probing questions about their strategies and the reasons for any errors they had made;
- observation notes of a sample of children working with a set of activities and tape-recording their conversations over a period of eight weeks.

(Continued)

In her data analysis, Valerie presented:

- the pre- and post-test results in the form of a graph, which clearly indicated the changes in children's scores;
- an analysis of different strategies and the reasons for children's errors using evidence provided in interview transcripts;
- Valerie's own personal list of significant issues and descriptions, which emerged during the intervention programme, outlining on-going changes in strategies.

Valerie reported her key findings under different themes, drawing on the information from all the data she collected – the test results using a graph, analysis of the content of her interviews about the type of strategies used by children in a table and her own observations in a working log.

Example

Action Research Project 3

Introducing Critical Thinking into a secondary classroom

As part of a set of one-year projects funded by the local education authority, Damien's action research project was to introduce a Critical Thinking course to his class of Year 7 (12 year old) students. He undertook this project as part of his professional doctorate in Education at university. In general terms, he organized his data collection based on his general aims for the project. He articulated the following as his broad aims for the study:

Education is quintessentially an intervention process designed for the transformation of outlooks and the development of skills for the benefit of both the individual and society. I believe Critical Thinking can be an effective instrument of that intervention process. Laudable claims relating to the benefits of inclusion of Critical Thinking in the classroom curriculum and its potential to contribute to developing logical thinking and its propensity to become incorporated in the study of traditional subjects are made in the literature I reviewed. The environment of many of the students in my classroom is dominated by the media and celebrity culture. Motivation to study is lacking in most of the students and the school truancy rate is high. The mastery of core curriculum subjects and changes of attitudes may result from the inclusion of Critical Thinking. Just as pebbles thrown into a tranquil pond send ripples generating motion beyond their place of landing, the introduction of Critical Thinking may be effective in producing results which transform these students' learning skills, test results and attitudes.

Damien's research question involved exploring the effectiveness of a Critical Thinking programme on the learning trajectories and attitudes of his students. In order to monitor the effectiveness of the intervention he adopted the following data collection methods:

(Continued)

(Continued)

- An open-ended questionnaire for all 31 students in the class to complete, asking them how they perceived their newly introduced Critical Thinking lessons.
- A sample of 12 students was interviewed, using a semi-structured interview format.
- Test results, pre- and post-project, in mathematics and English (provided by the UK National Curriculum and Assessment body). It was decided that the test results for a parallel class of children, due to receive Critical Thinking lessons in the following year, would be collected which could form a comparator group.
- Dated samples (three per term) of students' work in mathematics and English to monitor changes in quality, strategies used and grades given by the subject teachers.
- Interviews with subject teachers – at the end of each of the three terms – who taught mathematics and English to the intervention group.

Students had two 45-minute sessions of Critical Thinking each week for eight months. Damien also kept a journal where he recorded his comments after each lesson. He regularly analysed his notes on the basis of the objectives and noted some emerging themes as the project progressed. The first set of notes suggested that he was interrupting the students too much. In them he made the comment that constant interruptions did not give the students much opportunity for independent thinking, to 'exercise their metacognitive skills' as he described it, which was one of the objectives of the Critical Thinking course. He realized this and in his action plan for the next lesson, he decided to tell the students that he would be talking less when they were working on their tasks, but was happy to be asked for support and help when these were needed. He also assured them that he would be happy to listen to any individual or group who wanted to share their ideas with him at any time. In the fourth session Damien noticed that his interruptions were less and that the students stayed on task for longer. They also took the initiative more and generated new ideas. However, he was still concerned that his input was too restricted and wanted to take a more active part during children's discussions. So he asked a colleague to observe one of his lessons and to discuss ways forward. He also found some literature on Critical Thinking which gave him more insights into the objectives of the Critical Thinking lessons, such as encouraging processes of reasoning, seeking evidence and critically appraising one's beliefs. With an increased understanding of aspects of Critical Thinking and more support from his colleagues Damien planned the next few lessons, in the true spirit of action research which affords changes to be made as action proceeds.

When analysing all the data he had collected for his action research project, he included his own dated diary entries of how he saw his own teaching of Critical Thinking change over the period of the project. At the time of Damien's final data analysis and writing-up all the quantitative results were used alongside the themes

(Continued)

(Continued)

that had emerged from the qualitative data and these were presented in his thesis. Damien's final report also charted his own journey through the project and he discussed his professional development through his experiences. Unexpected themes that emerged and new questions that arose were also reported.

Analysis and presentation of your data

Let us now consider some general issues about how you would analyse and present your data. I will provide some specific examples of how our three action researchers described above (ARP1, 2 and 3), with two carrying out small-scale research which generated relatively small amounts of data and the other collecting more extensive data, had analysed and presented their data. Before you begin to represent your data you need to consider what kind you have collected. As I mentioned earlier, it is likely that you have collected some quantifiable data alongside your qualitative data (as is the case in each of our three examples), but in many cases all the data collected may be qualitative and in the form of interviews, field notes and researchers' diary entries.

Working with quantitative data

In your action research you may have collected some quantitative data which could help to supplement and complement the qualitative data you will be collecting. In action research projects that are located within your professional situation and practice (which will often form part of your Master's or professional doctoral work), you are unlikely to have collected a massive amount of quantitative data. You should be able to analyse and represent the quantitative data using frequency counts which you can represent in tables or using charts. A computer package such as Excel is suitable for this purpose. If an action research project involves several sites and the data are extensive, you may consider using a statistical packages such as SPSS (http://SPSS.com). Support in using this package would be given on your research training course. (A selection of useful reference books and websites is provided at the end of this chapter.)

Including charts and diagrams is worthwhile for two reasons. First, a visual display makes it easier for readers to understand the information. Secondly, these break up continuous prose which can sometimes be tedious for readers trying to make sense of numerical data. In a research project which explores the type of questions asked in a classroom, a researcher may present the information as a frequency table which is easy to understand. This type of information can also be presented in graphical form. When data are displayed in a graphical form, it is important to remember not to emphasize the findings in percentage terms as you are only studying small numbers. Making claims in percentage terms does not make much impact when you are only referring to a total number of 10 or 20!

Another simple bit of advice I have here is that whatever method you choose to analyse and display your data, you must tell your story effectively. Graphs and charts can look quite impressive, especially when in colour. Recently one of my students presented some data he had collected in both table form and through a number of colourful bar charts, which just repeated the same information in a visual format. When I pointed this out he was quite disappointed and a useful discussion followed about which form of representation was likely to communicate his findings more effectively to readers. Using tables is a simple and effective way for communicating your findings. As in the earlier example in Table 6.1, make sure you provide clear titles, label each column and give a clear indication of the total numbers involved and what the headings mean. It is often useful to ask colleagues (preferably those who have not been involved in the project) to look at your tables to be certain these make sense and then to make any adjustments as necessary.

Some examples of how two of the teacher-researchers (projects 2 and 3, described earlier) presented their data are shown below.

Table 6.2   An extract from an analysis of children's strategies for working on the place value of number on pre-project interview (Project 2)

Question: I have 256 sweets. How many bags of ten can I make from them?
Child I

Child: 25. It is easy. You cross out the last number and the rest are tens.
Teacher: How do you know that?
Child: My brother taught me; it is a trick.
Teacher: Do you know why the trick works?
Child: No.

Child 2
Child: I have to count, 10, 20, 30, 40, 50, 60, 70, 80, 90, 100, it will take too long. I give up
Teacher: Is there any other way you could work it out?
Teacher's comments:
Out of the six children I have interviewed so far, none of them have shown an understanding of the grouping concept of a number. I expected them to know the correct answer which many of them didn't. Even the child who gave me the correct answer – 25– used a rule which does not provide a sensible strategy or a basic understanding of how numbers are made up. I must take account of this in my teaching and show the number structure using groups of ten bundles of matchsticks to represent the number 256 and discuss the composition of the number with the group.

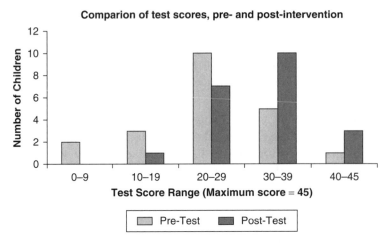

Figure 6.1   Children's pre-and post-test scores (Project 2)

Teacher's comments

Judging from the changes in total scores from the pre-to post-test, the teaching intervention using practical materials and a discussion of the structure of the numbers seems to have achieved some success. I need to compare the pre- and post-project interviews to see if children's strategies and understanding have changed. My observations suggest that there are some changes in children's thinking about numbers. They seem to use more mental imagery.

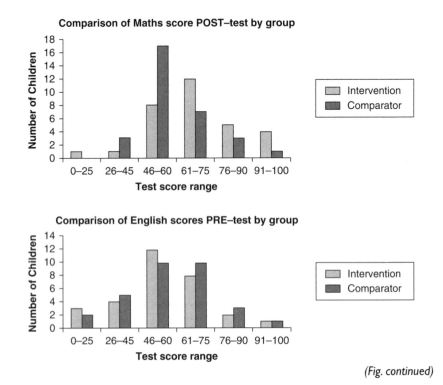

(Fig. continued)

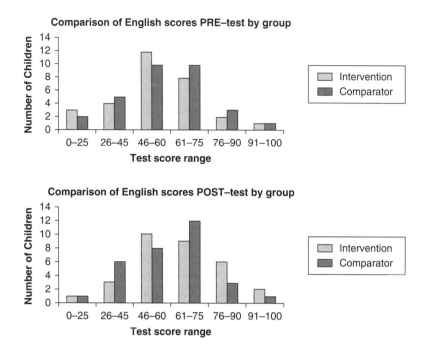

Figure 6.2   Test scores in mathematics and english of both intervention and comparator groups (Project 3)

Teacher's comments

The analysis of the results is facilitated by both groups consisting of 31 pupils – although one pupil was absent, for the English pre-test, in the Intervention group. In mathematics, the Intervention group showed significant improvement in the range 61 to 100; this was not the case with the Comparator group, although three improved to be in the range 61–90. In English there was also significant improvement in the Intervention group – the seven scoring under 45 became three in the post-test and the three in the 76 to 100 range became eight in the post-test. In the Comparator group no increase in scores 76 to 100 range occurred and seven remained in the less than 45 scores.

Working with qualitative data

As your action research is usually located within your professional context and practice, you would be exploring attitudes, behaviour and feelings which will necessitate the gathering of qualitative data, which you will need to analyse and interpret. The data you collect are likely to include open-ended question-naires, interviews, observation notes, personal logs and so on, most of which will be in the form of descriptive text. In the case of qualitative data, analysis of the text will involve you making an analytical framework which can often be subjective so it needs careful addressing in terms of reliability and validity (validating your research findings is discussed in some detail later in this chapter). If you have a large volume of text, the task of analysing all of this can seem daunting, but the positive angle to this is that in an action research project the qualitative data from various sources will help you to gain insights into the social reality of situations through the interpretations you make. If you have a considerable amount of descriptive data, one option you have is to use a computer package (as outlined later in this chapter) which is relatively simple to use. As a thorough account of computer packages is beyond the scope of this book, you could use the Further Reading section included at the end of this chapter to assist you on these.

Analysing qualitative data

There is no single correct way for analysing qualitative data, but one important factor that makes all data analysis effective is the need to be systematic. As I mentioned earlier, your data analysis may well have started when you organized and carried out your data collection. The type of questions you asked, the framework that you used for your observations and the nature of the documents you collected would have been structured in such a way that you used some themes and categories as part of this process. A step-by-step approach I usually suggest to my students is as follows.

- Organize your data, listing the different sets of data you have collected.
- 'Read the content; this is to get a general feel of what the data are telling you and how this relate to what you set out to do. All your data – observation notes, field diaries, policy documents and so on – need to be looked at. Common words and themes should start to emerge.
- Highlight sections in the data which are relevant to your research area.
- Construct categories to gather evidence. When you report your findings you will need to use actual evidence (numbers, actual quotes, artifacts, etc.) from your data to back up your claims. For example, if you interviewed ten children and eight of the transcripts of those interviews provided evidence of the effectiveness of your classroom intervention, you will need to make it clear that eight out of the ten children interviewed provided evidence that one of your aims had been met. This would enhance the trustworthiness of your findings.
- If you have a range of data to analyse, generate *codes* for analysis. (Coding is dealt with in later sections of this chapter.)
- Review the coded documents and select the significant themes to report.
- Interpret your findings.
- Validate the findings.
- Write your report and plan the dissemination.

A framework for qualitative data analysis and interpretation

If you have collected a significant amount of qualitative data, you should find Creswell's (2009) framework for qualitative data analysis and interpretation a

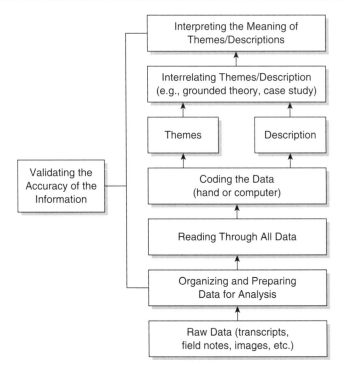

Figure 6.3   Data analysis in qualitative research (Creswell, 2009: 185)

very useful guide (see Figure 6.3). Creswell points out that 'preparing the data for analysis, conducting different analyses and moving deeper and deeper into understanding' is like 'peeling back the layers of an onion' for qualitative researchers.

The step-by-step approach proposed by Creswell provides a very useful guide for practitioners undertaking action research. I have summarized this in the following section.

- **Step 1.** Organize and prepare the data for analysis. This involves transcribing interviews, scanning material, typing up your notes and sorting and arranging the different types of data.
- **Step 2.** Read through all the data. A first step here is to obtain a general sense of the sets of information and to reflect on their overall meaning to get a first impression, from the ideas and their tone about the overall depth, credibility and use of the information. Make notes in the margin and record general thoughts at this stage.
- **Step 3.** Begin detailed analysis with a *coding* process. Coding is the process of organizing the material into chunks or segments of text before bringing meaning to information (Rossman and Rallis, 1998). Creswell's suggestions on what to use when coding are: code what readers expect to find based on past literature and common sense; code what is surprising and unanticipated; code for the unusual which may be of conceptual interest to readers. You

could hand-code the data, use colour code schemes and cut and paste text segments onto cards. The other option at this stage is to use a computer software package to help to code, organize and sort the information. (See the next section for the use of computer software.)

- *Step 4.* Use the coding process to generate a description of the setting or people, as well as categories of themes for analysis. Creswell suggests that you generate five to seven categories. These need to appear as headings and so will be useful for creating these. Support these with quotations and specific evidence.
- *Step 5.* Decide how the description and themes will be *represented* in the qualitative narrative. The most popular approach is to use a narrative passage to convey the findings of the analysis. This might be a discussion that mentions a chronology of events, a detailed discussion of several themes (complete with sub-themes, specific illustrations, multiple perspectives from individuals, and quotations) or a discussion with interconnecting themes. Visuals, figures, or tables as adjuncts may be used together with this discussion.
- *Step 6.* This final step involves making an interpretation or deriving meaning for the data. Questions about what lessons have been learnt are asked. These lessons would be based on your interpretations. They can also take into account information gleaned from literature or theories that confirm or diverge from them and to suggest new questions which may not have been foreseen earlier in your study.

Reflexivity and qualitative data

If your study involves mostly qualitative data collection and analysis, the issue of reflexivity needs to be considered when reporting your findings, as your own social identity and background may impact on the research process. For example, reflexivity is important for a teacher-researcher who is planning and implementing action in a classroom, while he or she is also a teacher. In such circumstances, that researcher needs to reflect on the possible impact of being a practitioner-researcher and acknowledge the possible influence this may have on the interpretations he or she makes and any bias which may influence the research process. As Creswell (2009: 177) points out, qualitative research is interpretive research with the enquirer typically involved in a sustained and intensive experience with the participants, which 'introduces a range of strategic, ethical and personal issues into the qualitative research process' (Locke et al., 2007).

Strengths of qualitative data within action research

As a final reflection on the use of qualitative data, I would stress that qualitative data have some particular strengths for the action researcher. In a very illuminating textbook focusing on qualitative data analysis, Miles and Huberman (1994: 10) indicate the features of qualitative data which contribute to its strength 'as its focus on naturally occurring, ordinary events in natural settings, so that we have a strong handle on what "real life" is like'. The authors describe the quality of its 'local groundness', as the data are collected in close proximity to a specific situation. What also makes qualitative data very suitable for the action researcher, according to the authors, is their ability to capture the 'richness' and 'holism' of a situation.

Using computer software

Using computer software for analysing qualitative data is another option available to action researchers. However, as Mertler (2006) points out, it is a misconception to think that the software will do the analysis as data analysis still requires the use of inductive logic which can only occur in the human brain. He reminds us that even advanced technologies cannot take the place of human logic. What computer packages can do effectively is help you to store and organize the data if these are typed. Packages can also provide a system for coding and categorizing the data electronically from all the notes and transcripts, thus enabling you to search for key phrases and words. However, if you are undertaking a project which involves collecting a large amount of qualitative data, using computer packages may be a good option. Most universities will provide both access to the packages and training on how to use them.

Coding

One means of organizing and understanding your data is to code the text. Coding is simply identifying the main themes and patterns within your data. Its purpose is for you to conceptualize and reduce your data down (Strauss and Corbin, 1998) into a manageable format from which to make conclusions.

There are many ways to code. Whatever method you choose, the most important things to bear in mind are your research questions and research aims. After transcribing all of your interviews, or immersing yourself in any of your other data sources, it is highly likely you will feel somewhat overwhelmed. There are two main feelings about your data which you may have to battle with. Firstly, you may think that all of what you have collected is important and relevant, which will consequently lead to the panic induced at the thought of having to leave something out (Auerbach and Silverstein, 2003). Coding should reduce this feeling, as once you begin to look for similar themes and patterns the data will feel much more manageable and it will become clearer as to what the relevant issues are. It is likely that you will think it is all interesting but once again it is important to remember your research questions and aims; if the data are not relevant to your aims they are therefore not relevant to you currently but these may raise new questions and suggest future directions for other research. Once you begin to realize you are coding only those things which are relevant, you will begin to feel in control of your data sets.

Coding can be hard work, but the tedium of coding can be overcome through techniques similar to those used when revising! Take regular breaks in order to maintain your full concentration, as well as frequently reviewing your coding criteria.

Many forms of data can be coded, although the most common is interview transcripts. It is also possible to code the open-ended responses to question-naire and survey results, as you would with the more closed-ended questions.

Example of coding for analysing an interview

After the analysis (see Figure 6.4) which suggested that Critical Thinking sessions may have an influence on students' outside life (Rebecca's interactions with her mother), Damien decided to send a short questionnaire to the parents/carers to find out more about the possible influences of teaching Critical Thinking on the students' lifeworld. Damien also decided to keep a record of the students' atten-dance (following the last sentence in the interview) and to compare the atten-dance of the intervention group to that of the comparator group.

Computer Aided Qualitative Data Analysis Software (CAQDAS)

Computer software for aiding the qualitative textual analysis process has been around for quite a while, but it is only in the last two decades that researchers have begun to realize its full potential and make it part of the normal research process. During the 1980s a wide range of packages was developed and today there are still over 20 to choose from. Traditional coding used very simple and traditional tools, pencils and coloured highlighters. The introduction of CAQDAS has brought transparency and discipline into qualitative analysis (Gaskell, 2000). (See also Kelly (2000) who has written an illuminative chapter on computer assisted analysis in Gaskell (2000)).

As there are so many CAQDAS programs this section can only mention those most commonly used and the particular programs found within the training courses offered by universities. These are only brief guidelines on how these programs can assist you with your data analysis; there is a vast array of specialist books on the market which can provide more detailed step-by-step guides as to how to use each program, some of which are listed at the end of this chapter.

NVivo

NVivo is the most recent textual analysis programme to be produced by QSR who made a name for themselves with the programme NUD*IST, which was

This is an example of the process of analysis undertaken by Damien who carried out the action research project on Critical Thinking which was included earlier in this chapter (as Action Research Project 3). The following short extract is from an interview transcript which was analysed by coding as a first step. It was further analysed using subcategories. Damien is interviewing Rebecca, one of the students in his intervention group. You may remember his objective for the project was to make an appraisal of the possible influences of teaching Critical Thinking. For this first analysis, he used the following codes to guide him through the process. You will see the coded issues underlined in the text.

LR   Learning related to the student
TR   Issues relating to teaching
OSB   Possible influence on learning other subjects
ATT   Change in attitudes
MTV   Relating to students' motivation
UEX   Not specifically related to original aims (or unexpected)
ORG   Organizational issues

Text as highlighted below

Codes	Text
	D: So what do you think of the Critical Thinking lessons?
ATT	R: Most of us thought first … Yeh, another lot of work in school and homework. Why can't we just do what we are doing now? Then, I started thinking, yeh, it is not bad really and I started enjoying the lessons.
	D: Tell me what did you enjoy?
	R: Well, for a start, we had a chance to talk to each other, discuss like and share what
LR	we thought instead of the teacher asking us questions and us answering them. We were allowed to ask questions about things like what do we think of adverts on the
TR	tele and not get the teacher cross all the time for asking. You know what I mean, not thinking that we were being rude or anything.
	D: Tell me more. What else do you think the lessons are doing?
	R: We think about things more. Kind of look at both sides of a story … like the murder story we did when we were asked about who was guilty and about
LR	prosecuting someone. We had to come up with good reasons for accusing someone
TR	for a crime. This is helpful
	D: Does that help you?
	R: In history lessons like … when we are asked to write an essay about the life 60 years ago, it kind of makes you think more.
	D: That is interesting, do the lessons help you in any other way?
OSB	R: I suppose, I have a go at things now and think well yeh, there are lots of ways of doing something. Like in maths lessons, I feel more confident
ATT	like … not worrying about saying the wrong thing.
	D: Why do you think you feel more confident?
MTV	R: It is what you say to us, if you can justify something that is cool … I do this to my mum now. When she asks me to do something or not to
ATT	do something, I give her some arguments and say she has to justify why she
TR	is telling me not to do something. I get into trouble sometimes, but I think she
UEX	feels pleased that I am more confident.
	D: So, do you think it is good that we started Critical Thinking lessons?
TR	R: Except one thing, by the time you get all warmed up and get into producing an
ORG	argument or preparing your points the lesson finishes … I don't know why we can't have the two lessons together, instead of two lessons a week. But it is nearly all good, I haven't missed any day in school when we have a Critical Thinking lesson.

Figure 6.4   Example of coding for analysing an interview

developed in the 1980s and has been changing ever since (Bazeley, 2007). To my knowledge, NVivo is the most widely used qualitative textual analysis software, with several institutions running training courses on it, and is often taught on Master's programmes.

Atlas.ti

Atlas.ti is another computer-based software item which enables researchers to organize text, graphics and audio and visual data files, as well helping with the coding of text.

Using evidence and generating knowledge

When I discuss data analysis with my students, we start with the question 'Why do we gather data?' The main purpose of gathering data is to provide evidence. In order to provide evidence you need to analyse the data you have collected. Again, the starting point will constantly remind you of what you are really looking for. You set out your aims at the start of your research and planned your data-gathering carefully, which has given you a good starting point for also gathering evidence for articulating your claims as well as for building your personal theories.

Whether you have collected quantitative data or qualitative data or a combination of the two, it is important to remember that ultimately the value of your research will depend on the quality of the type of data you have collected, the interpretations you make and your personal reflections and conclusions. The significance of your project will depend on the way you have collected and analysed your data.

During data analysis, whether you do this manually or using a computer package, it will be useful to highlight those parts which you could use as evidence when you make claims and share your research. With my students, I suggest that they colour code different types of evidence under sections: how the original aims were met, what problems were encountered during the project in terms of practical day-to-day events, as well as methodological aspects. Your personal learning, its implications and the practical significance of the research for yourself and others – as well as any new questions and research directions – could also be noted. In your final report you will need to include all of these.

So what do I mean by providing evidence? Take the example of the action research project introducing Critical Thinking to the class of 12 year olds and the monitoring and recording of any changes in aspects of the children's learning, such as their motivation, attitudes, quality of responses, engagement in discussions and general confidence. Data were also gathered on the students' performance in tests and compared with that of another group. Data also included students' test results in mathematics and English, attendance, pre- and post-intervention open-ended questionnaires, interviews with a small sample of students and notes from the observation of lessons which was carried out with a colleague. Here the researcher's initial aims were based on the hypothesis that students will display changes in learning strategies and attitudes. He would need to constantly remind himself of these aims during data analysis and when collecting evidence to assess if these were happening as a result of the intervention. He would not only be making notes on emerging themes, but also gathering extracts of evidence for these. Unanticipated, nevertheless important outcomes of the research and their implications would also be noted.

Generating knowledge

The purpose of research is to generate new knowledge and in your case the knowledge produced is based on your practice – all aspects of it – and planning, what you have read, your data collection and what you have found out. You will have to articulate the knowledge you have generated, how it has affected your practice and what significance it may have for other practitioners. Here you are building personal theories based on what you have done. The personal theory arising from the example relating to the introduction of the Critical Thinking project was articulated as 'by asking the children to engage in Critical Thinking processes, I have been able to enhance their confidence in tackling all aspects of their work, as my colleagues who teach them other subjects also tell me' and 'I think by giving children time to keep a personal reflective diary this helps them to evaluate their work' and so on. Thus your theories will emerge from your practice. You have contributed to knowledge and have provided illustrative examples of what happened in your classroom and quoted relevant evidence. The claims you make and the theories you formulate are original, as you have employed your own critical thinking skills and judgement skills. Remember that in order to make valid claims to knowledge, you will also need to back up your claims with evidence using relevant parts of your data; this may consist of extracts from interview transcripts, selected sections from your notes of classroom observation, artifacts, photographs and examples of children's work. (Some of my students include learning trajectories and profiles of pupils, with dates, to show the changes.)

Validating your claims to knowledge

Your research findings and claims to knowledge will be more powerful if you validate them. Action research is mostly carried out in collaborative teams involving communities of enquiries (see Chapter 2); this makes it easier to seek common understandings and interpretations so the findings are more representative. The trustworthiness of your research is also judged in terms of how your claims to knowledge are accepted by those who read your reports and published articles. So how do you validate your claims to knowledge, bearing in mind the readers who will evaluate them critically? For the purpose of validation the first step is to be able to articulate your procedures clearly, explaining how you conducted your research, how robust your methods of data collection were and how triangulation (see Chapter 5) was achieved. Expect to be challenged on all aspects of the research claims you are making.

I encourage my students to organize validation meetings with different groups of people who are able to consider their research processes and findings from different perspectives both during their research and at the conclusion of the project. For example, the first audience may be fellow researchers during a seminar presentation. This may be less daunting, but the danger is that fellow researchers don't always ask you harsh questions as they have a particular empathy for your situation and don't want to give you a 'hard time'. The teacher-researcher (cited earlier) who undertook the project on introducing Critical Thinking presented his findings to a group of local education district advisers who had responsibility for teaching and learning. If you are based in a school, your audience could consist of colleagues (try to include those who were not part of the project), teacher support teams and parents or school governors who will bring their own perspectives into discussions and debates. Inviting colleagues from neighbouring schools, especially those who have similar roles and responsibilities within their institutions, is also a good strategy. At the time of reporting your research, you must include details of your validation meetings and what transpired in these.

It is useful to set up a group of Critical Friends when you establish the project. Explain to them that their role is to evaluate all aspects of the research by challenging your assumptions and to help you consider ways of reducing the inevitable subjectivity and ethical issues and the usefulness and replicability of your research. It is useful to circulate documents to Critical Friends to read and comment on individually and to give you formative feedback at different points of the research, as it is not necessary to have group meetings all the time. Writing up summaries of these meetings is useful to you to keep monitoring the quality of your action research, especially to check on the following aspects.

- Are you focused on your research aims or questions?
- Are your action plans clear and realistic?
- Are you aware of any ethical considerations?
- Are the data collection and analysis procedures robust?
- Do you have appropriate evidence for the claims you intend to make?
- Are you able to demonstrate critical awareness?
- Is the research likely to contribute to new knowledge?

☐ Summary

This chapter focused on the data analysis which preceded writing up your report and the publication of your findings. Various forms of data summaries were presented. Using examples of action research projects undertaken by three practitioners, aspects of organizing, analysing and representing data were addressed. A framework for qualitative data analysis was provided, along with a discussion of the extraction of the themes and patterns emerging from the collected data. Issues of reflexivity were considered. The use of computer software in data analysis was briefly discussed. The chapter concluded with a discussion of the importance of using evidence and generating and validating knowledge before claims are made.

 ## Further Reading

Auerbach, C.F. and Silverstein, L.B. (2003) *Qualitative Data: An Introduction to Coding and Analysis*. New York: New York University Press.

Bazeley, P. (2007) *Qualitative Data Analysis with NVivo*. London: SAGE.

Creswell, J.W. (2009) *Research Design: Qualitative, Quantitative, and Mixed Methods Approaches*. Thousand Oaks, CA: SAGE.

Gaskell, G. (2000) 'Individual and group interviewing', in M.W. Bauer and G. Gaskell (eds), *Qualitative Researching with Text, Image and Sound*. London: SAGE.

Huberman, A. and Miles, M.B. (1998) 'Data management and analysis methods', in N. Denzin and Y. Lincoln (eds), *Collecting and Interpreting Qualitative Data Analysis*. Thousand Oaks, CA: SAGE.

Kelly, U. (2000) 'Computer-assisted analysis: coding and indexing', in G. Gaskell (ed.), *Qualitative Researching with Text, Image and Sound*. London: SAGE.

Strauss, A. and Corbin, J. (1998) *Basics of Qualitative Research: Techniques and Procedures for Developing Grounded Theory*. Thousand Oaks, CA: SAGE.

7

Writing up your
action research

This chapter focuses on:

- the process of writing up action research;
- the structure of dissertations;
- using case studies for presenting action research.

I will start this chapter with a quotation from one of my Master's student's work which captures the spirit of what I want to say in this chapter. Ann wrote:

> For me writing a report of my action research was a very special time. It was like telling someone the story of my professional journey. It was a time for further reflection on what I had learnt and understood and also about forming a vision of other horizons. The process of writing an account of what and how I did my research brought it all together for me and it was very rewarding. Writing the final report made me realize that I have emerged from the experience of action research feeling more confident and enlightened. Not only that I found out much more about aspects of my practice and new directions to take, I also realized that I have become more curious and ask more questions ... (Ann, primary school teacher)

Like many other teacher-researchers, Ann carried out an action research project on a topic which arose from her intrinsic motivation to improve her practice. She also selected this study for her Master's dissertation. She was expected to write up a report for her school; she found the whole process of writing this report for her school and for her dissertation a rewarding experience. Not all action researchers are expected to produce written reports, but for those who are in the process of producing a final report of their action research useful guidance is provided by Hopkins (2002: 140), who asserts that all action researchers need to put their data together in such a way that:

- the research could be replicated on another occasion;
- the evidence used to generate hypotheses and consequent action is clearly documented;

- action taken as a result of the research is monitored;
- the reader finds the research accessible and it resonates with his or her own experience.

At this point, I can reflect on my own experiences in my role of supporting action researchers in a variety of contexts. After carrying out their studies for several months or for a whole year, depending on their circumstances, it was time for them to produce a written report for their institution or sponsor or for the purpose of obtaining a qualification.

Writing a report of your action research

Whether you are writing this report as part of the requirements for an accredited course or for the purpose of just making it available for others to read, here are a few factors to consider. Remind yourself that the mode of study that you have selected is action research and the purpose of action research is to improve practice or to implement change, as a result of your research, as part of professional development. Your intention, as an action researcher, is not to make generalisable claims, but to tell your story which should be of interest to other practitioners who may wish to learn from it, or replicate the study, or apply your findings to their own situations.

What kind of report?

From the outset, it is important to consider the audience, the requirements and the purpose of your report.

Consider your audience

Ask yourself: who is my audience? You may have obtained funding from an external source for your action research and in such cases you may have been given a specific format to follow. The case studies of teacher-researchers reporting their findings, funded by the Teacher Training Agency in the UK in 1997, all started with the following four common subheadings and then the writers selected their own subheadings for the rest of the report which were appropriate for the topic of their enquiry.

- Aims.
- Dimensions of the case study.
- Summary of findings of the case study.
- Background.

It may be that you are writing a report or dissertation as part of the requirement for a qualification. In this case, your dissertation will be read by academic tutors and sometimes by an external examiner. If this is the purpose of your report you will be expected to follow a particular format and the conventions of scholarship. In a long study or a dissertation you will also be expected to show your knowledge of recent and relevant research literature. Whatever the purpose, it is important to be clear and consistent and demonstrate a good understanding of the issues you are researching. In the case of a dissertation for accreditation purposes, the expectation will be that the study is extensive as you would be considering yourself an expert in your chosen area of study. While reporting an action research, the quality of your writing can be enhanced by writing in an authentic and personal style. I have always felt that reporting action research is often powerful for one's own professional development because of the personal nature of the writing. It is helpful to remember that you are reporting your own story, one that you have constructed from your experiences and collaborations with other people.

Think of the reader

A useful strategy to adopt when writing your report is to consider any potential readers of your report. The following guidance may be of help.

- Always provide the background to your study and your context as an action researcher. This helps readers to relate to your report and possibly apply the findings to their own circumstances.
- It is important to present your aims at the outset and present your findings within the context of what you have set out to achieve.
- Readers appreciate realism and honesty. It makes sense to report what has progressed smoothly as well as any difficulties you may have experienced.
- Present your plans and outlines of action clearly. It is possible that others may want to replicate what you did or report your findings to their colleagues.
- As action research is often a personal journey, writing the report in the first person is more effective. Sentences such as 'I chose this method because I had the opportunity to study this as part of our school-based professional development ...' or 'I changed direction after finding out ...' makes the text reader-friendly and more accessible.
- Don't assume that readers will always be knowledgable about what you are discussing. Try and explain all aspects of your study in clear, simple language. Keep your target audience in mind. If the report is going to be read by parents and governors it would be inadvisable to use the kind of education jargon which you may have effectively utilised before to disseminate information to your colleagues.
- Use subheadings where possible. It is easier to read text with subheadings.
- Be creative in your presentation. This is possible within any given format. Some of my students use thought bubbles, cartoons and photographs containing evidence when they present their findings.

Writing a Master's dissertation

In this section I will try to provide some guidance on writing a dissertation based on your action research. This is not, by any means, meant to be a definitive document. I don't believe that a fixed set of rules can ever be applicable when you write up action research, because at the very heart of an action research project is the opportunity to be flexible, emergent and creative. However, if you are writing a dissertation for accreditation purposes, you will need to follow the format given by the institution. Within that set format, there will still be plenty of opportunities to be original.

A dissertation is the culmination of the work you have undertaken which should demonstrate to readers your personal understanding of an issue, what actions you have taken and how these actions have informed and developed your professional life. The emphasis is on personal learning and not in providing generalisations about education.

As your study is likely to be an enquiry into your own practice, you need to pay attention to the following:

- Acknowledge your own beliefs, prior assumptions and values at the start of the report (see Chapters 1 and 6).
- You need to acknowledge your inevitable subjectivity upfront.
- Say, at the outset, that the interpretations are personal and how you established trustworthiness and validated these.
- State clearly what methods were used for data-gathering and how multiple perspectives were sought.
- Discuss any ethical issues and how these have been addressed.

Maintaining quality

If you have a set of criteria for grading your dissertation, you must read them first. The following general checklist should help you to monitor the quality of your work. Have you:

- made your aims and objectives clear?
- justified why you are undertaking the work – providing a rationale?
- acknowledged your own perspectives and beliefs?
- made the context clear ? (This is important as action research, in most cases, is located within the distinct situation of a practitioner.)
- demonstrated your understanding of issues relating to the topic?
- shown that you have made efforts to read work carried out by others in your area of research and any theoretical literature relating to your study?
- explained how you collected the data and how you have made efforts to triangulate and validate the information?
- presented the data in an accessible manner and in such a way that readers can identify the evidence you have generated for your conclusions?

- made coherent arguments?
- demonstrated your personal learning?

All dissertations should also demonstrate the following features:

- a clear formulation of the research question or topic of study;
- a *critical* account of theories and research, including your own viewpoints and commentary;
- justified methods of enquiry;
- clearly presented data;
- ethical procedures;
- a robust analysis of data;
- generated knowledge based on evidence;
- a discussion of the findings and emerging issues;
- a reflection on both your findings and the methodology used;
- the limitations;
- the enhancement of personal knowledge;
- a reflection on personal action and future directions;
- an organized bibliography.

Structuring a dissertation

As mentioned previously, higher education institutions will usually provide a basic format for writing a dissertation. A close study of the formats issued by a few institutions showed that although there were differences in the words used to describe the different parts of a dissertation, they all seemed to require a similar content. In the following section, I will present a set of guidelines that I provide my students. These are in the form of chapter headings for writing a dissertation (with approximately 15,000 words in total). These guidance notes may be adapted for all courses leading to a qualification. Remember, I am referring to the format of a dissertation which arises from carrying out an action research project.

Abstract

This section will provide a short summary of the aims, methodology, findings and implications for practice. This must be *brief* – about 200 words should be sufficient. I ask my students to complete their abstract on two sides of a postcard and show it to me before they write this up. Many of my students will finalise their abstract after writing the rest of the dissertation – this is wise because during the writing-up process your thoughts will come together and help you to present an effective abstract. Do remember that the abstract is the first section of your study that is read by your supervisor or examiner and first impressions are important. Don't forget your study may be placed in the library, where others who are interested may read it. It is customary to use the past tense here, as you are reporting what has already been done.

Table of contents

Chapter 1 – Introduction

In this chapter you must set out the context of the study and discuss the reasons for undertaking it. What was the personal and professional motivation? Why at this time? What are the trends in the topic of study in terms of recent local, national or international developments, using some references to the literature? What specific aspect of the topic do you intend to study? If it is a research question, or hypothesis, present it clearly. New initiatives? What are your aims? This chapter also provides a guide, as signposts, for the reader about what to expect in each chapter; remember that this needs to be in a short, summarized form. (About 1,500 words)

Chapter 2 – Review the literature

This chapter should present the reader with a comprehensive review of the literature relating to your topic of study. References must be made to recent and relevant literature – theory and research – on your topic. Are there any current debates on your choice of topic? What has been written about the topic and who wrote it? I often ask my students to present the literature in themes. The ideas you have gathered from your literature search should be analysed. The purpose of this chapter is to locate your study within a framework informed by what is out there and what has already been found out. This is, therefore, an important chapter which needs careful planning and organization. Rather than listing each writer's views or theories, try to connect the different perspectives of different authors by drawing on the similarities and contrasts in their thinking. Presenting a summary of what each author has said, without pulling the ideas together, makes for tedious reading. Use subheadings where you can. Provide a critical commentary of your own on what is being presented. (About 3,000 words)

Chapter 3 – Methodology

In your dissertation you would acknowledge action research as your mode of study. Why did you choose action research? Here you need to discuss the features of action research which make it suitable for your study. What is action research? State your epistemological and ontological stance briefly and explain how the methodology fits in with your philosophy. Discuss very briefly how action research evolved, over the years, as a method of enquiry for practitioners. What models of action research do you know about and what is your understanding of these models? What are the advantages of action research as a method? Relate these specifically to your project. Show the reader that you are also aware of the limitations of action research and respond to these in terms of the study you are about to embark on. You should describe the design of the study and the preparations and planning that preceded taking action. How did you collect the data? Did you use observations? Interviews? Videos? Diaries? Why did you select the methods? Justify your choices and also show that you are aware of the limitations of each method you used. Ethical considerations should be included in this chapter. (About 2,500 words)

Chapter 4 – Action and data collection

For this chapter you may use a different title such as 'Activities', 'What did I do?', 'Implementing action' or 'Gathering data', or any other phrase which you feel most appropriately reflects what you did for your project. In this chapter you must give sufficient detail for others to understand what you have done. Bear in mind that they may want to replicate your project. Explain your data-gathering methods, your first trials and report any modifications you had to make. This chapter has to contain detailed narratives of what you did, highlighting the outcomes using a range of techniques. Transcripts of tape-recordings, observation notes and references to photographs can be used to provide evidence for any claims you choose to make later. Your aim is to present a detailed and effective account of what happened during the action stage and to present your findings. If you revised your action, you may want to refer to the succession of action cycles within your action research. Don't forget to justify how you addressed the issues of validity and reliability. Who did you share your data with? Did you use Critical Friends or colleagues to achieve triangulation of your data? (About 3,000–4,000 words)

Chapter 5 – Analysis of data and results

How did you analyse your data? What did you find out? Represent your findings effectively and clearly. Include evidence to back up your claims. Extracts from tape-recordings, observations and personal logs may be used. Documentary evidence can also be presented. What has changed? Your claims must always be supported by robust data. (You may find it useful to follow the guidelines provided in Chapter 6 of this book.) The findings you present in this chapter must inform the reader of the impact your project has made. (About 2,500 words)

Chapter 6 – Conclusions and discussion

What are your conclusions? What themes have emerged from your study? How does it relate to your professional situation? Do your findings reflect what others have found out? Has your study generated evidence which contradicts the outcomes of studies carried out by others? In this chapter, you need to give an account of your own personal learning. Reflect on the outcomes of the project. What personal theories can you make on the basis of your study? What contribution has your study made? How will your findings influence your practice? What are the implications of your research for you, your institution and for others? Were there any parts of the study which posed problems? What do you think of your methods of data collection? Were they suitable? List and discuss any limitations of your study. What future direction does the study suggest? (About 3,000 words)

Bibliography

Appendices

Test your understanding of a dissertation structure

Below is an exercise which should help you to internalise the structure of a dissertation.

The following extracts are taken from the MA dissertation of a student who obtained high marks from an external examiner, which was written using the above format. The title of the dissertation was: 'The role of speaking and writing in mathematics as a way of enhancing mathematical understanding'. The personalised and reflective nature of the writing was given special credit. (Note that full references were provided in the original dissertation but these are not reproduced here.)

Try to write down the number of the chapter where you think each of the extracts appeared. For obvious reasons the chapter extracts are not in any special order. I have provided a list of the actual chapters where these appeared, at the end of this section, so please cover these until you have completed your answers. I must remind you that this is an example of just one dissertation, and that this format may not be suitable for all reports. I hope it will still help you to think about the structure and style of writing of a dissertation or report.

A. My interest in the topic began when I listened to a lecture on the role of language in mathematics. I felt excited and wanted to find out more about it.

B. Here I acknowledge the inevitable subjectivity in interpreting the data. But I feel reassured by the fact that action research allows me to draw personal insights from this project. Any claims I make are only applicable to my study. However, others who read this report may be able to identify features which are applicable to them.

C. I found out that literature on mathematics communication is sparse, especially in the United Kingdom. I found Brissenden's argument that communication and discussion in mathematics are essential ingredients in promoting mathematics learning very convincing. His views are similar to what Vygotsky (1976) ... My own experience with children has shown ...

D. Natalie, age 9, emphatically told me that you only write diaries in English lessons. The conversation I taped during a lesson with a group of four children provided evidence of their perception of mathematics as a discipline which is about numbers and doing sums. Here is an extract from Natalie's conversation with me.

Teacher: What I would like you to do is to keep a mathematics diary for the next few weeks, where I would like you to write down what you have learnt and what you think of a lesson.

Natalie: But, miss, we keep a diary for our news every week. Isn't diary writing for English lessons?

Teacher: What makes you think that a diary is only used for an English lesson?

(Continued)

(Continued)

Natalie: Because, mathematics is really all about numbers. We do sums in maths lessons. How can I write a diary in mathematics? There is nothing to write. You don't talk in mathematics. Do you? …

E. The key questions I wish to investigate are:

- Can more discussions in mathematics lessons enhance children's mathematical understanding of concepts?
- What changes may occur in terms of children's confidence and attitudes by introducing more talk and writing in mathematics lessons?

F. What I am still not sure of is how one can promote mathematical talk when you are under pressure to cover a crowded syllabus. Government documents encourage discussion, but I am always thinking that a natural flow of unconstrained discussion is in conflict with teaching for tests. I will need to resolve this …

G. Looking back at my study, I realize how my practice has changed in terms of making my questions more open-ended. An analysis of the type of questions I had asked the children showed that I didn't really give them many opportunities to talk, I was too passive myself …

H. As part of my action research, I planned two types of intervention. This I will refer to as my first cycle of activities. Monitoring the effects of these interventions, I knew I would be able to plan other activities or modify my ideas.

I. One of the findings which emerged was the increased level of confidence demonstrated by the children. Their talk quite often reflected a higher level of learning. As I began to discuss more in their group time, they started using more sophisticated language and seemed to better understand the concepts relating to the words. What I discussed in Chapter 2 with reference to Vygotsky's (1978) Zone of Proximal Development highlighting the role of an adult scaffolding children in supporting their learning was in evidence …

J. What have I learnt? Changing my practice was a challenge. For years, my own perception of the nature of mathematics had been that it was a structured but lifeless discipline consisting of numbers, four rules of number and correct answers. I needed a lot of guidance before I could embark on this project. But the result was worth the effort. My perceptions have changed and this was brought about by watching my children grow in confidence. Both my children and I now 'speak' mathematics …

K. My way forward is to share my ideas with my colleagues. I would feel that I have not really completed my story until I have told it to some more people and find out if they feel as excited about it as I do …

L. The methods I used had to be appropriate for the context I am working in. I was a class teacher. I had an opportunity to undertake a project based in my classroom. I could collect information by listening and observing my children. I also had access to their written work which I could monitor over a period. Then I also needed an ongoing record of my experiences. I could clearly see what Carr and Kemmis (1986) meant by action research offering real opportunities for reflecting on practice based on evidence. I drew up an observation schedule and justified the value and advantages of this method of collecting data in a real setting …

Now that you have completed the task, I can tell you where in Deborah's dissertation the above extracts are from. I have reproduced more extracts from Chapter 6 as most researchers find this part of the writing more challenging.

A – Chapter 1   G – Chapter 6
B – Chapter 3   H – Chapter 4
C – Chapter 2   I – Chapter 6
D – Chapter 4   J – Chapter 6
E – Chapter 1   K – Chapter 6
F – Chapter 6   L – Chapter 3

Doctoral theses

If you are undertaking Doctoral work, using an action research approach, the framework for your thesis may still be similar to that of a Master's dissertation, but a higher degree of critical engagement with the existing theory and literature and a greater depth and conceptual analysis will be expected. You will also need to articulate your philosophical and theoretical perspectives in greater detail. Here is an extract from an abstract from a doctoral student undertaking action research in her institution.

Abstract

This thesis presents the processes and outcomes of an action research project undertaken in my professional context. The project was based in my institution. I explain the background of my situation and my personal motivation for carrying out the project. The choice of action research as a methodology is justified as it provides me with greater flexibility so as to refine my practice based on emerging findings. My contribution to 'living knowledge' is based on the on-going dialogue with my colleagues and the community of enquiry we created. My non-positivist, interpretive stance is justified in terms of my epistemological and ontological position on the basis of which I selected a qualitative methodology ...

Creative presentations of action research

Here I draw on my experience of working with action researchers who have used very creative ways for presenting their findings. Some practitioners presented their research findings to colleagues and others at conferences before writing their final reports, as they believed that the preparation for the presentation helped to bring their thoughts together. Others presented their research outcomes after writing their reports. Some of the researchers did not actually write a formal report but disseminated their research in other ways, which still served the purpose of bringing their ideas together and reflecting on them before sharing their work with others. So what forms of presentations are possible? Here are some examples of how you may present the outcomes of your action research. You will find more information on presentations in the next chapter.

Displays

Andrew, a secondary school teacher, displayed the outcomes of his research on introducing Critical Thinking to his students as an exhibition at the local teachers' centre. The titles for different sections of his display were:

Main title: Introducing Critical Thinking to 12 year old students
Subtitles:

- What is Critical Thinking?
- Why use Critical Thinking with students?
- Critical Thinking in action
- What did the children say and do?
- What did I observe?
- High and low days
- What did my colleagues think?
- My thoughts on the influence of Critical Thinking on student learning
- What did I learn from carrying out the project?

The exhibition gave Andrew plenty of opportunities to display his evidence and pose questions and include his own reflective commentary (in thought bubbles). With the rapid advancement of software packages these days, it is possible to create impressive displays.

Conference presentations

Another way of disseminating action research is for researchers to make presentations to interested audiences. Three examples of such presentations, arising out of projects I have guided, come to mind. One was the presentation of a project by a group of teachers, also guided by two local district advisers, to explore ways in which talented young children's emotional needs could be met. The teacher-researchers shared their project at a national conference, with an audience of 120 Early Years practitioners. Using PowerPoint slides and clips of video recordings, these presenters brought their project to life. The story being told by class teachers, using powerful images, added to the interest in the project, which led to many of the participants wanting them to share their experiences in local venues.

The second presentation at a national conference – researching the possibility of introducing the well-known Italian Early Years 'Reggio Emelia' programme in Early years classrooms in the UK – involved a university academic in working with a group of teachers. This too led to considerable interest among practitioners who either wished to participate in the project or replicate it in their local contexts.

The third presentation of a mathematics enrichment project was produced by two practitioners, alongside a group of children, who convincingly and passionately demonstrated the impact of an intervention study on children's learning and attitudes. They used examples of video clips of work, transcripts of interviews and a series of *before* and *after* images of the improvement in their spoken and written work.

Telling a story as a case study

In recent times many case studies of action research have been posted on websites. Within the interpretive and emergent methodology of action research, the process of writing case studies can often help a researcher to reconstruct a convincing story. These stories are often found to be more accessible to readers than research reports, thus true to what Walker (1986: 189) describes a case study as

> A study of particular incidents and events, and the selective collection of information on biography, personality, intentions and values [which] allows the case study worker to capture and portray those elements of a situation and give it meaning.

As I mentioned in Chapter 5, I feel that writing case studies is an ideal way of disseminating action research, as it can offer a meaningful story to readers in a style suited to those who are interested in the practical implications of an action research project.

☐ Summary

This chapter dealt with report writing which can often be the final stage for action researchers. After the choice of topic, cycles of enquiry, data collection and analysis, the end is in sight. The report is the ultimate activity serving the purpose of portraying the action research as your attempt to investigate a phenomenon and disseminate the findings on which to base further practical changes. Your target audience, its interest and disposition need to be borne in mind. Although dissertations have to follow specified structures provided by institutions, a general set of guidelines for writing dissertations was provided. A collection of extracts from a dissertation was given to help you relate to the style and content of a dissertation. Writing a Doctoral thesis, using on action research approach, needs to follow a more flexible structure in order to take the emerging nature of the action and the findings into account. One example of an abstract from an education doctorate student, who carried out an institution based study, was included. The possibility of disseminating action research findings as case studies, exhibitions and conferences was also discussed.

Further Reading

Baumfield, V., Hall, E. and Wall, K. (2008) *Action Research in the Classroom*. London: SAGE.

O'Leary, Z. (2004) *The Essential Guide to Doing Research*. London: SAGE.

McNiff, J. and Whitehead, J. (2005) *All You Need To Know About Action Research*. London: SAGE.

Mertler, C. (2006) *Action Research: Teachers as Researchers in the Classroom*. Thousand Oaks, CA: SAGE.

Yin, R. K. (2003) *Case Study Research: Design and Methods*, 3rd edition. Newbury Park, CA: SAGE.

 Useful websites

- Research Informed Practice Site (TRIPS) – www.standards.dcsf.gov.uk/research
  - A UK government website providing summaries of the latest research and case studies.
- National Foundation for Educational Research – www.nfer.ac.uk
  - Provides research summaries and reports of recent research projects.
- *Action Research* – www.actionresearch.net
  - An academic journal which publishes studies of interest to action researchers.
- www.triangle.co.uk
- Collaborative Action Research Network – www.did.stu.mmu.ac.uk/carn
  - Provides details of research publications and research conferences.
- *Educational Action Research* – www.tandf.co.uk/journals
  - Gives details of the above journal.

8

Publishing your action research and planning the next steps

This chapter focuses on:

- why you should disseminate the outcomes of your action research;
- the various ways of dissemination;
- publishing in professional circles;
- publishing in academic outlets.

In the previous chapter, we focused on you writing up your research, with particular reference to writing dissertations. We will now explore the theme of sharing your research with others, in greater detail, in this chapter. Carrying out action research is an intrinsically satisfying activity. After much reading, planning and evaluating, you have completed your research and it is time for sharing the new knowledge you have generated with others. While you were carrying this out, it is highly likely that you were informally sharing your experiences with colleagues at your institution and other professionals in the local area. If your research has been funded by an external body, the funder will expect you to send in your report. If a research grant has been provided, the research funding body may expect you to disseminate your findings at research conferences and to write a few papers for publication in academic journals. In this chapter I will try to offer more practical guidance on how to share your findings in a range of ways; both locally and globally.

Many of the practitioners I have worked with on action research projects feel they don't have much to say to others. Sometimes they will say that writing is only for academics in universities and will lack the confidence to embark on this course. During my conversations with practitioners who have carried out action research, the following issues have been raised as acting as barriers to them publicising their research.

'Surely, it is doing the research which is important, not the writing.'

'No one is going to take note of what I have to say. I don't have the background or the expertise to publish.'

'Who will take note of what we, the teachers, have to say? No one will read it after all that effort.'

Whilst I empathize with the misgivings and feelings of inadequacy felt by many, I have also shared the pleasure that many of the practitioner researchers feel when they do make conference presentations, contribute to a newsletter, publish their findings on a website or put their papers in professional or academic journals.

So why do I think it is important to publicize your action research? First, disseminating your personal learning and what you have found out is important for your professional development. The process of writing up your research and sharing it with other professionals and academics encourages the further construction of knowledge and reflection on your ideas, reinforcing your understanding and helping to ground your ideas. Teachers who have worked with me on action research projects have often felt a sense of worth and pride when they find out that their publications have been read by other professional colleagues. Second, of course, is that publishing your research provides evidence of your own professional development and achievement and this addition to your curriculum vitae can often help towards promotions and progressing in your career.

Where will you disseminate your findings?

Having decided to publicize your research more widely, the next question to consider is how you are to go about making it a reality. Your research can be communicated in various forms. You may write a report about your research project, or discuss it in a newsletter for colleagues in your local area, or submit it to your own school's newsletter for parents and governors. Publishing your research on a website is also common these days; this can be an effective visual medium for presentation and you may choose to include an interactive element in it, so that you will be able to invite feedback and comments from other users. This contributes to on-going learning and the sharing of ideas, as you become part of a collaborative network of professionals communicating their ideas with each other. Your research may be communicated at national and international conferences or you might wish to disseminate your findings through a few of the above outlets. The various different forms of dissemination will require careful planning as you need to consider the different audiences and appropriate styles for the various ways of dissemination you decide to make. Let us now consider some ways of publishing your research.

Writing a research report

To add to what we discussed in the previous chapter, here is some more detailed guidance. In a research report you will be outlining the whole process of carrying out your research, how it was conducted, what you found out, your conclusions and the possible implications of your conclusions for practice (and, if appropriate, for policy makers too). The length of your report will vary with the nature of the project, such as the length of time it took and the source and level of funding you received. It is useful to look at examples of reports on websites; most government websites will publish reports of funded projects. For example, in the UK, the Department for Children, Schools and Families government website publishes reports of various projects undertaken by practitioner researchers. Writing a report helps you get your thoughts down on paper in a coherent manner: from there you should be able to use that report as a basis for other forms of writing by adapting it to suit different formats and audiences. In the following section I have included a conventional format for a report based on one written by a practitioner colleague in a school as part of the requirements for a funded project. It had 76 pages in total. As you can see, it is an easy format to follow.

Executive summary

The executive summary can consist of about four (A4) pages. It provides an overview and summary of the whole content and guides the reader through the various sections of the report.

Introduction

You need to tell the reader about the background to the research and its context. Why was it undertaken? It may be that you were initiating a new policy, or addressing an issue in your institutional development plan. It is possible that you were commissioned by policy makers to undertake the research. Make sure you include details of any published literature or documents which sets the scene.

Aims

You must state your aims and objectives clearly; what you were hoping to find out or achieve.

Review of relevant literature

The length of this section and what you include here needs to be decided in relation to the total length and your audience. It would be useful to include a list of the recent and relevant documents and readings you consulted when you were carrying out your action research.

(Continued)

(Continued)

Planned activities

Provide a list of the activities that you planned for the project. This section will be very useful and of significant interest to other practitioners who may wish to replicate your project in full or using parts of it. Include the sources for any published materials you used. Details of what you may have designed for the project and your rationale for using these materials will be useful also.

Mode of enquiry

Your mode of enquiry would be action research in the context of this report. Give details of the sources for data used and how any ethical issues were addressed (see Chapter 5). Brief details of how the data were analysed should be included.

Findings

Your main findings should be listed and supported by evidence. You may have various tables and figures to include, but extracts from interviews, field logs, quotes from colleagues and documentary evidence such as pupil's work and photographs will make the report interesting and more accessible for the practitioners who will constitute your main audience.

Conclusions

You must say what your conclusions are relating to your aims.

Implications for practice and policy

Here you need to comment on the implications for other practitioners. If you are researching a policy issue, your report will be of interest and significance to policy makers. You may also consider making recommendations for both practitioners and policy makers, as appropriate.

Professional newsletters

Professional newsletters may be in a written format, if they are to be distributed to colleagues in local area or to parents in a school. These could also be placed on an institution's website which then makes these accessible to large audiences through search engines sharing your research globally. In all cases, it is important to have your audience in mind. For example, a newsletter for parents needs to be very focused and relatively short, providing a summary of what was done and what the outcomes were. On the other hand, a newsletter for professional colleagues – in print or on the website – can be longer, as your readers would want to know more details about the project and where they can get more information, if they wish. The need for clarity and a visually pleasing presentation cannot be overemphasized here. In this section you will see an example (with kind permission from the researcher) of what a teacher-researcher included in a newsletter written for a practitioners' network. The author wrote this for dissemination to her colleagues, based on the research report which she sent to the trust which funded her action research. This report provides a considerable level of detail which should be of help to you.

Case Study

Specialist Schools and Academies' Network
My Action Research – Introducing Challenge in the classroom

Carole Portman Smith, Whitton School, UK

Context

Whitton is an 11–16 years mixed comprehensive school located on the Richmond/Hounslow borders. Fifty per cent of students come from outside the education district of Richmond upon Thames, many from the neighbouring district of Hounslow. I drew on principles from the work of Professor Joyce Van Tassel-Baska at the Centre for Gifted Education, College of William and Mary, Williamsburg, USA, after I attended a conference where she spoke. Van Tassel-Baska's work focuses on how to deliver a challenging curriculum in the classroom for gifted students. Her paper 'Challenges and Possibilities for serving Gifted Learners in the Regular Classroom' identifies the major obstacles that prevent teachers differentiating for gifted learners in regular classrooms. She introduced us to two curriculum models they use with schools. I felt that her findings are as relevant to our school in the UK, as they are in the schools surveyed in the USA.

My Action Research Question: Can we use Van Tassel-Baska's 'thinking models' to increase the level of challenge for gifted students within subject areas?

Van Tassel-Baska (2003: 6) has noted that the 'use of systematic challenging curricular intervention is often lacking in schools and that planned curricular experiences have not been sustained over time'.

Sample and Methodology

Action Research was my mode of enquiry. I followed a plan–act–evaluate–reflect–refine cycle for my project. I defined the word 'Challenge' and my colleagues were asked to ensure that students had a shared understanding of the concept.

   The student sample was an 'opportunity sample' which was the current Year 9 (aged 14) accelerated Science group. This gave a 95 per cent match to Year 9 students on the gifted and talented register (top 10 per cent) in the school. It was not possible to

(Continued)

(Continued)

work with the entire top 10 per cent from the register, as this cohort would have been dispersed across a large, unmanageable number of sets across subjects.

The sample selected was all within the same sets for maths, English, science and other subjects where staff had volunteered to take part in this project. This made communication with students easier.

Pre- and post-project student questionnaires were used to find the perceived level of challenge and the responses to this. This was designed with a mix of open questions to probe students' thoughts and feelings and some closed, multiple choice questions. The limited time available for this project has been a major factor in selecting the methods used. Students and teachers were also asked to complete a short evaluation form at the end of lessons where the models had been used. Teachers collected work samples to provide additional evidence of the responses to the challenge set.

Parents and teachers were also given a pre-project questionnaire to provide a snapshot of our starting point.

Following staff training and the trialling of models, I also conducted focus group interviews to review the impact and issues around the use of the models.

Ethical Considerations

All staff, parents and students involved were made aware of the project and its aims. Student questionnaires were completed under the 'student voice' element of the school's personalised curriculum. This is a system that was already well established within the school. It is designed to collect students' opinions and to allow them to have a say in their own education.

Research Activity

The project involved staff from a range of different subjects using pre-selected models to help develop higher-order thinking skills and creative and critical thinking within the same teaching group. The intention was to develop these skills alongside advanced subject specific content. Perkins and Salomon (1989) provide evidence that there is better transfer of learning when higher-order thinking skills are embedded in subject matter. Teachers were asked to look at the topics being taught during the period of this project and to suggest where the subject matter lent itself to the use of a specific model.

The project aims were modified following initial findings from the questionnaires filled in by teachers, students and parents at the start of the project. The final aims were:

- to use Van Tassel-Baska's models to promote deeper learning and increased challenge within subject-specific lessons;
- to discover if teachers and students perceived an increased level of challenge during these lessons;
- to encourage collaborative learning;
- to encourage students to view challenge and failure as learning opportunities.

(Continued)

(Continued)

Outcomes

As this project involved a small sample of 33 students and was context bound, it is not possible to generalize the results. However, the processes involved and principles adopted offer possibilities for replication.

1. Tasks Set

Seven out of the eight teachers who took part in the project designed sessions using the models. The Modern Foreign Languages (MFL) teacher found this quite difficult, however she was very creative and took ideas away from the training sessions and designed tasks which required students to construct sentences and a paragraph of writing from groups of words provided in a word bank. Students were then required to explain how they had produced their final piece of writing, thus introducing metacognition (thinking about thinking) into the task to make it more challenging. This 'working backwards' theme was further developed in a mathematics session where students started with the solution and then worked backwards to formulate the question. Three members of staff also used ideas, gained from the way in which the models were presented, to plan other activities which developed higher-order thinking skills of analysis, synthesis and evaluation. In mathematics, a sequence of tasks was developed to increase the level of challenge and record students' responses to this.

English, science, geography and religious education teachers also designed tasks using the models to develop critical thinking skills.

2. Student Responses

Students were asked to rate their perceptions of the level of challenge according to the scale shown here; these are subjective and acknowledged as a limitation of the study. However, most students felt able to do this given a shared definition of the word 'Challenge'. One member of staff noted that the students who made little effort to complete the task were often the ones awarding a grade 1 or 2.

1. Very easy, no help needed
2. Easy, no help needed
3. Requires a little effort and no help
4. Requires a little effort and some help
5. Requires a lot of effort and some help

Initially, students awarded a mean score of 2.7 for lessons before the project started. Initially, only nine students (less than 33 per cent) said they were sufficiently challenged to need help. Gifted students develop their learning by being taken outside of their comfort zone; they require 'scaffolding' to construct their own knowledge and make sense of their learning. It is possible that this support was being provided by friends, alternatively, it could be provided without them realizing it. A third explanation is that they were simply not being sufficiently challenged to reach their full potential. This initial score of 2.7 can be compared with scores awarded at the end of each lesson delivered as part of this research project.

(Continued)

(Continued)

MEAN SCORE = 2.7 (pre-project)
MEAN SCORE = 3.6 (post-project)

An interesting theme emerged within open student responses to longer tasks. A number of students (five out of 28 in science) commented that the task was very time-consuming; one said 'I would not normally have time to do that'. Perhaps this is a reflection of students' inability to commit to a task; recent research suggests that task commitment and creative thinking are crucial to students' success.

Another theme, which was found across all the student evaluations, was the realisation that they were investing a lot of time 'thinking for themselves'. Comments included 'You had to use your brain', 'I found this fun, but I had to use my head a bit more', 'It required a lot of effort to find the information'.

Many students commented on how much they had enjoyed a 'challenge day'; nine out of 17 students, providing additional comments about the challenge day noted that it was 'fun or enjoyable'.

Every task also contained some negative comments such as 'boring' or 'took too long and not enjoyable'. These were always in the minority, a maximum of two negative responses from each set (25–30) of students' evaluations. It is possible that students did not wish to write their negative comments even though they may have thought them. All evaluations were anonymous to encourage honesty.

3. Teacher responses

Responses were generally positive; seven out of eight teachers taking part considered the project to be useful in raising the level of challenge in lessons. Teachers were asked to use the models within topics, already planned during the project timescale, so as not to create extra work or artificially create situations where the models would be useful. The maths and MFL teachers found it the most difficult to incorporate the models into their teaching. However, they adapted lessons using the ideas presented on higher-order thinking and presented sessions where they had delivered content in a different way to the usual. Student feedback illustrated an increased perception of challenge within these lessons. In addition to increased challenge and the development of higher-order thinking skills, staff identified the following learning opportunities when working with the models.

- Collaborative learning.
- Metacognition – reflecting on how a task had been completed.
- Consolidation of knowledge when used as extended plenaries and for revision.
- Understanding how an idea fits into a bigger picture.
- Skills transfer across subject boundaries.
- Making evidence-based decisions.

(Continued)

(Continued)

- Exploring new ways of learning.
- Promotion of a greater tolerance of the views of others.

Conclusion

Within the limitations of this small-scale project, the results seem to indicate that there has been an increased level of challenge within lessons, often delivered by tasks which involved higher-order thinking skills. The two key components of the project – the provision of resources (models) and time to discuss and share good practice – may have influenced the success of the project, as a lack of resources and time is often a barrier to differentiation.

References

Perkins, D. and Salomon, G. (1989) 'Are cognitive skills context bound?', *Educational Research*, 18: 16–25.
Van Tassel-Baska, J. (2003) 'Challenges and possibilities for serving gifted learners in the regular classroom', *Theory into Practice*, 44(3): 211–217.
VanTassel-Baska, J. and Little, C. (2003) *Content-based Curriculum for the Gifted*. Waco, TX: Prufrock Press.

Publishing in professional journals

By writing in a professional journal you will be sharing your research – both the research process and your findings – with education professionals. You need to use the sort of information you have included in your report, but in a different style to engage your readers. Again, share the sources of the materials and resources you have used or designed, with examples, because busy practitioners appreciate having access to tried and tested materials. Using case study examples and anecdotes makes your story more powerful and reader-friendly. When you share your experiences as an action researcher, don't forget to include any possible problems you may have encountered, which adds to the realism of carrying out research as part of your professional work. Unanticipated problems and barriers to progress are common within the realities of classrooms and institutions. Writing collaboratively or with a 'writing mate' makes the process less stressful. Look for specialized journals using professional association websites. For example, if your project is concerned with improving children's reading, an English Association website will give you a list of their publications and, similarly, mathematics and science associations or special education networks will provide a list of their journals. Have a look at the style of the articles published in a journal before you write your draft. It is often helpful to produce a summary of your research and send it to the editor of the journal, asking whether they would be interested in considering your article for publication. In my experience journal editors of professional journals are very keen to publish work from practitioners who constitute their main readership. Practitioners who work with us at the university often tell us that they see the experience of writing papers for professional journals as a useful first step towards writing papers for academic journals. You will also find a number of journals which publish action research. The editors of such journals would be keen to publish good quality projects. Remember if you look inside a copy of any journal, there will usually be details of who to submit your work to for consideration.

Making oral presentations at professional conferences

Presenting your findings at conferences organized by professional associations or government organizations (these may have specific themes) is another way of sharing your research findings with professional colleagues. Practitioners who worked with me on various action research projects have enjoyed making conference presentations to colleagues who have always shown considerable interest in action research projects which are practical in nature. During oral presentations, we can often see the researchers' passion in the work they have undertaken and their enthusiasm is infectious. Based on oral presentations I have attended, I have constructed a set of guidelines which may be of use to you. It may be that you already know these, or that you will find them useful.

- If you are making a PowerPoint presentation, make sure you only include pointers on the slides and do not read from the slides; the audience would like to hear you speak about your experiences. Keep eye contact at all times. It is a pleasure for others to see teacher-researchers getting animated whilst narrating their stories.
- Make the presentation interactive and depending on the time allowed give the participants some short tasks which relate to your project. This keeps the interest and attention of the audience.
- Use case studies – these can be about children or situations. Case studies may include short films and photographs and these act as documentaries.
- When you present your evidence and outcomes, in addition to any charts and figures you may use, show examples of children's work, extracts from interviews and comments from evaluations.
- Don't automatically assume that practitioners don't like to know about your theories and the research you have used in your project. Provide an overview of these. It gives you more academic and scholarly credibility. It is also useful to give out a sample of readings and a set of references, at the end of the presentation.
- Finally, give your audience an e-mail address so that they can contact you for further information if they wish to. If you don't mind visitors to your institution to see what you have done, extend an invitation also.

Publishing in academic outlets

It may be that you have decided to present your research at a research conference or write a paper for an academic journal. Here are some useful points to help you to achieve this.

Who is your audience?

First you need to consider who your audience is. If you have an international audience, you need to be careful about the terminology and language you use. Make the context of your work clear. Try to avoid the acronyms and abbreviations used in one country which may not be understood by an international readership.

Presenting at academic conferences

Assume you wish to make a presentation at a research conference. The first step is to look at the websites of research associations such as the British Educational Research Association (www.bera.ac.uk) or the American Educational Research Association (www.aera.net). Both conferences have SIGs (Special Interest Groups) for action research or practitioner research. A few presentations on action research that I have attended at the AERA conference were from practising teachers reporting research within their institutions; these attracted large audiences. The above websites will give you information on the different formats for presentations that you can submit. For example, at both the conferences you can submit individual papers or poster presentations. At the BERA conference new researchers are strongly encouraged to present papers and this may be an option for your first paper to be presented. You will be asked to provide an abstract with a fixed number of words using the format provided. For the AERA conference submissions, you will be asked to address the following in your proposal.

- Objectives or purpose of the project.
- Perspectives or theoretical framework.
- Methods, techniques, or modes of enquiry.
- Data sources or evidence.
- Results and conclusions.
- Educational significance of the study.

Once your paper or poster is accepted you will need to expand these headings for your presentation at the conference. In many cases a paper that has been accepted for presentation will be suitable for publication in an academic journal. Every time my colleagues and I have presented papers at the AERA conference, journal editors who have been present in the audience invited us to submit papers to their journals for publication.

Another useful place to look at is action research network websites (see the end of this chapter) which announce various conferences. They may also be interested in publishing your contribution.

Writing a paper for an academic journal

If you decide to write for an academic journal, then the following steps could be taken.

Preparation stage

- Have a look at the websites of academic journals to see some samples of journals and published papers. Most university libraries have educational journals and if you are a student at one or working with a member of the university's staff you should be able to get such journals on-line. The journals which publish action research (see the end of this chapter) are likely to be very interested in publishing your work.
- Download abstracts of papers which interest you.
- Make a note of what a journal is looking for. Read the guidance notes in the journal which will outline its aims, the audience, format and style and the suggested wordage.
- Select the most suitable-one or two journals for submitting your research output.

Writing a paper

You may find the following guidance helpful.

- *Prepare an abstract.* This is a short summary of what your paper is about. Why did you do what you did? How did you do it? What knowledge was generated and what would you like your colleagues or the rest of the world to know about your work? Some people suggest that you do your abstract last, but I always find it useful to have a postcard summary of what I am going to be writing in the paper as an abstract before beginning to write that paper and to then revise it after this is completed. You can access sample abstracts and sometimes the full text of papers from journal websites.
- *Write your draft paper using the format of the particular journal you have in mind.* Make sure you stay focused and articulate your theoretical stance. Show that you have researched what others have found out in areas related to your research. Robust methodology and the collection and analysis of data are important aspects that reviewers will look for. Finally, it is most important to highlight what new knowledge your study has contributed and its significance to education.
- *Complete the references and bibliography.* If you can use an automated referencing tool such as 'Endnote' this will make the task easier.

- *Get a Critical Friend (preferably someone who has not been involved in your project) to read your paper for clarity and language.* You may have links with the local university as part of your project, in which case you could ask the tutors to read the draft and make comments.
- *Revise the draft and send the paper to the selected journal for consideration.*

In most cases, journal editors will ask for some revisions to your paper and then it will be published.

A checklist for reviewing your paper before you send it for publication

I have often found the list of criteria used by research associations and journals very useful for reviewing my papers before I submit them. Rejections are part of the academic writing process, but you can enhance the quality of your paper by addressing the following questions.

- Have you clearly stated the background to your study and why the study was carried out?
- What type of study was it? In the context of this book, it would be using an action research approach. Why did you select this method of enquiry?
- What are your aims or objectives?
- Have you included an analysis of the theory and research which informed your study?
- Have you articulated your study design carefully?
- Are the methods of data collection and analysis clear?
- Has the study addressed ethical issues?
- Have you articulated the limitations of your study?
- What contribution has your study made to the existing knowledge base?
- Are there any special aspects of carrying out action research which the reader may find useful, in terms of personal learning or the process itself?

☐ Summary

This chapter focused on how you can publish your research findings to a range of audiences. Guidance on writing reports was provided, supported by examples. This chapter also dealt with aspects of disseminating your research in the form of newsletters and conference presentations to both professional and academic audiences. A detailed section on how to go about writing a paper for an academic journal was provided. The chapter concluded with a set of criteria which could be used as a checklist before submitting papers for publication.

Useful websites

- *Action Research* – www.actionresearch.net
  - An academic journal which publishes studies of interest to action researchers.
- American Educational Research Association – http://www.aera.net
- British Educational Research Association – http://www.bera.ac.uk
- The Collaborative Action Research Network – www.did.stu.mmu.ac.uk/carn
  - Provides details of research publications and research conferences.
- *Educational Action Research* – www.tandf.co.uk/journals
  - Gives details of the above journal.

Endnote

I wonder how many readers, when first approaching this book, had a view of academic researchers as esoteric dwellers in ivory towers in which their output simply accumulated dust. I hope you can appreciate by now that action research methodology has been steered throughout its evolution by some talented academics who were responsible for its conceptual instruments and refining their use. The major ongoing value of action research is in the hands of readers such as yourself. Action research methodology in the hands of practitioner researchers has become the DIY of education research. I would emphasize, however, that a successful engagement here requires you to be determined, industrious and yearning for transformations.

Writing this book has been a pleasurable journey for me. It has offered me the opportunity to reflect on the benefits of practitioner research for both the individual and for their institutions. I wish you luck in your own action research.

Glossary of key terms

Do you feel mystified by some terms in the research language? Here are some explanations. They are only meant as a starting point for you to investigate further, as you proceed with your research.

Action research. This is carried out by practitioners as part of a process of change. The research is context-bound and participative; it often uses a qualitative methodology.

Case study. A case study is an enquiry into a particular case or cases. You may seek data from multiple sources of evidence. The knowledge you generate relates to the case or cases you have selected, based on your understanding of the cases. Case studies often provide you with an in-depth knowledge of people, events, programmes and situations.

Coding. This is a process used for data analysis. It involves assigning a code to help you with the interpretation of segments of data.

Critical Friends. These are persons who will help to validate your data, descriptions and interpretations; these are considered critically before offering feedback.

Data. These form the information you collect as a researcher. You may generate a lot of data as tape-recorded interviews, questionnaires, field diaries and documentary evidence. It is very important that you design an effective, personal system to organize your data.

Data analysis. In general terms, this is the process of making interpretations of the data you have collected and, possibly, constructing theories based on your interpretations.

Documentary analysis. This relates to the process of analysing and interpreting the data gathered via documents. For example, government documents, school policies, and the contents of meetings, diaries or school records are studied and analysed to make observations.

Emergent quality. In action research, you will make adjustments to your plans in response to on-going assessments. The cyclic nature of action research allows you to take account of a quality which has emerged which was not exhibited in the previous cycle.

Epistemology. This concerns theories of knowledge and about how you come to know.

Ethics. This covers ethical principles and adherence to professional codes. These principles need to be at the centre of your data-gathering, data analysis and the writing-up of projects.

Field notes and field diaries. These are entries made by researchers based on their observations and thoughts. Field notes do not have to be in written form; audio tapes and video tapes can be employed to gather authentic data. In participant observations, using field notes can be particularly useful.

Objectivity. This is a complex term, but in practice it involves the avoidance of any intrusion of your preconceptions or value judgements. Objectivity is a means of avoiding bias and prejudice in your interpretations.

Ontology. This is the theory of being. It is the study of how things exist in the world, whether they exist subjectively, or independent of the observer.

Participant observer. If, as a researcher, you are involved in what is being studied you are a participant observer. In action research you are likely to be involved in the project as a participant observer.

Qualitative/quantitative methods. The simplest explanation is to describe qualitative data as being in the form of descriptions using words, whereas quantitative data will involve numbers. The debate as to which methods are more reliable goes on; I recommend that you select the methods which are likely to provide the appropriate data for your purpose.

Reflexivity. This is the process in which as a researcher you will reflect on your values, biases, personal background and situations in the shaping of your interpretations.

Reliability. You can describe a study as reliable if it can be replicated by another researcher. Careful documentation and the clear articulation of procedures can contribute to greater reliability.

Subjectivity. The personal views and the commentaries of you as a researcher can sometimes be viewed as bias, but do not have to be so. If you declare the possible subjective nature of your statements or personal judgements and provide justifications for them these can be powerful in constructing arguments within action research.

Triangulation. This is recommended as a way of establishing the validity of findings. Assume you collect data from multiple sources involving various contexts, personnel and methods. The process of triangulation involves sharing and checking data with those involved. This should lead to you being able to construct a more reliable picture.

Validity. In action research, validity is achieved by sound and robust data collection and the consensus of accurate interpretations. The latter is a contentious issue in my view as interpretations can be very personal in nature and achieving a consensus may not always be possible within action research. Different interpretations of a situation may add to a debate and lead to the personal and professional development of the researchers involved. In action research it is advisable to set up a **validation group** to consider a researcher's claims to knowledge. The role of the group is to consider the procedures and evidence against which the claims are made.

References

Adelman, C., Jenkins, D. and Kemmis, S. (1976) 'Rethinking case study: notes from the second Cambridge conference', *Cambridge Journal of Education*, 6(3): 139–50.

Auerbach, C.F. and Silverstein, L.B. (2003) *Qualitative Data: An Introduction to Coding and Analysis*. New York: New York University Press.

Bassey, M. (1998) 'Action research for improving practice', in R. Halsall (ed.), *Teacher Research and School Improvement: Opening Doors from the Inside*. Buckingham: Open University Press.

Bazeley, P. (2007) *Qualitative Data Analysis with NVivo*. London: SAGE.

Bell, J. (2005) *Doing Your Research Project: A Guide for First-Time Researchers in Education and Social Science* (4th edition). Buckingham: Open University Press.

Black, P. and Wiliam, D. (1998) 'Assessment and classroom learning', *Assessment in Education*, 5(1): 7–71.

Blaikie, N. (1993) *Approaches to Social Inquiry*. London: Polity.

Blaxter, L., Hughes, C. and Tight, M. (1996) *How to Research*. Buckingham: Open University Press.

Burrell, G. and Morgan, G. (1979) *Sociological Paradigms and Organizational Analysis*. London: Heinemann.

Carr, W. and Kemmis, S. (1986) *Becoming Critical: Education, Knowledge and Action Research*. London: Falmer.

Cohen, L. and Manion, L. (1994) *Research Methods in Education*. London: Routledge.

Creswell, J.W. (2009) *Research Design: Qualitative, Quantitative, and Mixed Methods Approaches*. Thousand Oaks, CA: SAGE.

Elliot, J. (1991) *Action Research for Educational Change*. Buckingham: Open University Press.

Elliot, J. and Adelman, C. (1976) *Innovation at Classroom Level: A Case Study of the Ford Teaching Project* (Open University Course E203: Curriculum Design and Development). Milton Keynes: Open University Educational Enterprises.

Ernest, P. (1991) 'Constructivism, the psychology of learning, and the nature of mathematics, some critical issues', in F. Furinghetti (ed.), *Proceedings of the 15th Conference for the Psychology of Mathematics Education*. Assisi, Italy: University of Genoa.

Gaskell, G. (2000) 'Individual and group interviewing', in M.W. Bauer and G. Gaskell (eds), *Qualitative Researching with Text, Image and Sound*. London: SAGE.

Hargreaves, D. (1996) *'Teaching as a research-based profession: possibilities and prospects'*, Teacher Training Agency Annual Lecture, April.

Hopkins, D. (2002) *A Teacher's Guide to Classroom Research*. Buckingham: Open University Press.

Kelle, U. (2000) 'Computer-assisted analysis: coding and indexing', in M.W. Bauer and G. Gaskell (eds), *Qualitative Researching with Text, Image and Sound*. London: SAGE.

Kemmis, K. and McTaggart, R. (2000) 'Participatory action research', in N. Denzin and Y. Lincoln (eds), *Handbook of Qualitative Research*. London: SAGE.

Levin, M. and Greenwood, D. (2001) 'Pragmatic action research and the struggle to transform', in P. Reason and H. Bradbury (eds), *Handbook of Action Research: Participative Enquiry and Practice*. London: SAGE.

Lewin, K. (1946) 'Action research and minority problems', *Journal of Social Issues*, 2: 34–46.

Lincoln, Y. (2001) 'Engaging sympathies: relationship between action research and social constructivism', in P. Reason and H. Bradbury (eds), *Handbook of Action Research: Participative Enquiry and Practice*. London: SAGE.

Locke, L., Spirduso, W. and Silverman, S. (2007) *Proposals that Work: A Guide for Planning Dissertations and Grant Proposals*. Thousand Oaks, CA: SAGE.

MacGarvey, L. (2004) 'Becoming marvellous', *Times Educational Supplement*, 11 June.

Macintyre, C. (2000) *The Art of Action Research in the Classroom*. London: David Fulton.

Mason, J. (2002) *Researching Your Own Practice: The Discipline of Noticing*. London: Routledge Falmer.

Mertler, C. (2006) *Action Research: Teachers as Researchers in the Classroom*. Thousand Oaks, CA: SAGE.

Miles, M. and Huberman, M. (1994) *Qualitative Data Analysis*. Beverly Hills, CA: SAGE.

O'Dochartaigh, N. (2007) *Internet Research Skills*. London: SAGE.

O'Leary, Z. (2004) *The Essential Guide to Doing Research*. London: SAGE.

Reason, P. and Bradbury, H. (2001) *Handbook of Action Research: Participative Enquiry and Practice*. London: SAGE.

Robson, C. (2002) *Real World Research*. Oxford: Blackwell.

Rose, R. (2002) 'Teaching as a "Research-based Profession": encouraging practitioner research in education', *British Journal for Special Education*, 29(1): 44–48.

Rossman, G. and Rallis, S. (1998) *Learning in the Field: An Introduction to Qualitative Research*. Thousand Oaks, CA: SAGE.

Schön, D. (1991) *The Reflective Practitioner*. New York: Basic.

Stenhouse, L. (1975) *An Introduction to Curriculum Research and Development*. London: Heinemann.

Stenhouse, L. (1983) *Authority, Education and Emancipation*. London: Heinemann.

Strauss, A. and Corbin, J. (1998) *Basic Qualitative Research*. London: SAGE.

Times Educational Supplement (2004) 'Classroom discoveries', Special Edition, 11 June.

United Nations Convention on the Rights of the Child (1989) *UN General Assembly Resolution* (44/25). Geneva: United Nations.

Von Glasersfeld, E. (1987) 'Constructivism', in T. Husen and N. Postlethwaite (eds), *International Encyclopaedia of Education* (Supplement Vol. I). Oxford/ New York: Dergaman. pp. 162–163.

Vygotsky, L. (1978) *Mind in Society*. Cambridge, MA: Harvard University Press.

Walker, R. (1986) 'The conduct of educational case studies: ethics, theory and procedures', in M. Hammersley (ed.), *Controversies in Classroom Research*. Milton Keynes: Open University Press.

Yin, R.K. (2003) *Case Study Research: Design and Methods* (3rd edn). Newbury Park, CA: SAGE.

Zeichner, K. (2001) 'Educational action research', in P. Reason and H. Bradbury (eds), *Handbook of Action Research: Participative Enquiry and Practice*. London: SAGE.

Index

Added to a page number 'f' denotes a figure.